PENGUIN BOOKS

MORE CHRISTMAS CRACKERS

John Julius Norwich was born in 1929. He was educated at Upper Canada College, Toronto, at Eton, at the University of Strasbourg and, after a spell of National Service in the Navy, at New College, Oxford, where he took a degree in French and Russian. In 1952 he joined the Foreign Service, where he remained for twelve years, serving at the embassies in Belgrade and Beirut and with the British Delegation to the Disarmament Conference at Geneva. In 1964 he resigned from the service in order to write.

His many and varied publications include two books on the medieval Norman Kingdom in Sicily, *The Normans in the South* and *The Kingdom in the Sun*, which are published by Penguin in one volume entitled *The Normans in Sicily*; two travel books, *Mount Athos* (with Reresby Sitwell) and *Sahara*; *The Architecture of Southern England*; *Glyndebourne*; two anthologies of poetry and prose, *Christmas Crackers* and *More Christmas Crackers*; *A History of Venice*, originally published in two volumes; his three-volume history of the Byzantine Empire, *Byzantium: The Early Centuries*, *Byzantium: The Apogee* and *Byzantium: The Decline and Fall*; and, recently, the single volume *A Short History of Byzantium*. Many of his books are published in Penguin. In addition he has written and presented some thirty historical documentaries for television, and is a regular lecturer on Venice and numerous other subjects.

Lord Norwich is chairman of the Venice in Peril Fund, Co-chairman of the World Monuments Fund and a former member of the Executive Committee of the National Trust. He is a Fellow of the Royal Society of Literature, the Royal Geographical Society and the Society of Antiquaries, and a Commendatore of the Ordine al Merito della Repubblica Italiana. He was made a CVO in 1993.

More Christmas Crackers

being ten commonplace
selections by

JOHN JULIUS NORWICH

1980 - 1989

PENGUIN BOOKS

for

Allegra

with thanks for past contributions
entreaties that she keep up the good work
and love

PENGUIN BOOKS

Published by the Penguin Group
Penguin Books Ltd, 27 Wrights Lane, London W8 5TZ, England
Penguin Putnam Inc., 375 Hudson Street, New York, New York 10014, USA
Penguin Books Australia Ltd, Ringwood, Victoria, Australia
Penguin Books Canada Ltd, 10 Alcorn Avenue, Toronto, Ontario, Canada M4V 3B2
Penguin Books (NZ) Ltd, Private Bag 102902, NSMC, Auckland, New Zealand

Penguin Books Ltd, Registered Offices: Harmondsworth, Middlesex, England

First published in one volume by Viking 1990
Published in Penguin Books 1992
5 7 9 10 8 6 4

The acknowledgements on p. 319 constitute an extension of this copyright page

Printed in England by Clays Ltd, St Ives plc

Contents

. . . how these curiosities would be quite forgott, did not such idle fellows as I putt them down.

John Aubrey

When, in the summer of 1970, I whiled away a rainy Sunday afternoon making a selection of twenty-four short items culled from my two commonplace books then existing, with the vague idea of devising a mildly original Christmas card for my friends, I little thought that this most agreeable task was to become an annual event – still less that it would continue for twenty years. But it was, and it did; which is why I now find myself sitting on a bougainvillaea-shaded terrace above the Mediterranean and writing an introduction to the second ten years of Christmas Crackers.

My introduction to the first decade – which was published in 1980 – gave a fairly full account of the genesis of the enterprise; in the unlikely event of there being any owners of this earlier volume who wish to refresh their memory, they need only read it again. For new readers, however, I should perhaps briefly rehearse the principal reasons why, over the past thirty years, the collection of short literary items of the kind to be found in the following pages has become one of the enduring pleasures of my life. The most important is that it occupies the minimum of space and costs precisely nothing: my only indulgence is the morocco-bound blank albums – there are now seven of them, identical except in colour – in which it is transcribed. I am ready to swear, none the less, that my excitement at every new trouvaille *is every bit as great as that of other more exalted collectors when they stumble on a Mauritian Penny Black or a rare first edition.*

But that is only the beginning. After the vital twenty-four-hour waiting period before passing final judgement on the latest acquisition (for a passage that looks marvellous one evening can seem surprisingly hollow in the cold light of day) there is the pleasure of finding it suitable neighbours. No commonplacer worth his salt starts boringly at the beginning of his album and works through to the end; in the early stages, I simply let the book fall open at random and copy the new entry at the first empty page, but as it gets fuller the quality of haphazardness has to be worked for. Finally comes the joy of transcription, in my very best handwriting, on to the virgin page. (Always a virgin page: if a new addition doesn't deserve that, it shouldn't be there in the first place.)

Since a commonplace collection is unaffected by monetary considerations, its only limitations are those which the collector himself decides to impose. It will thus reflect not only his taste, but his personality as well – which is why no two collections are ever remotely the same. One may show a preponderance of love lyrics, another of Wildean epigrams; all too many tend to go overboard with those nasty sanctimonious little aphorisms that used to appear in pokerwork over tear-off calendars. I nowadays try to avoid aphorisms altogether, together with anything too obvious (a common-

place book that begins with 'To be or not to be' and continues with 'If' will live up all too faithfully to its name); anecdotal jokes; stories that have to be told in my own words; and, in principle, anything found in other people's anthologies – though occasionally, and notably with the Notebooks of Geoffrey Madan – the temptation to piracy becomes irresistible.

As long as he obeys this last rule, the commonplace collector will be on his own, far from the world of experts and dealers, catalogues and salerooms. Indeed, one of the very first lessons he learns is never to go deliberately looking for material, for by doing so he negates the only certain criterion for eligibility: whether or not the item leaps off the page and spontaneously hooks his attention. The conscious search somehow blunts the antennae. The secret is never for an instant to forget that wherever two or three words are gathered together, there your quarry may be lying concealed: the art is to keep eyes and ears permanently cocked, and to hold yourself constantly ready for the spring.

This book does not mark the end of the road, any more than its predecessor did. In another ten years – if I live that long and anybody is still interested – I hope to produce yet another, just in time for the millennium. Sufficient, however, unto the day: this second milestone is more than enough to be getting on with. It is, essentially, a simple reprint of the last ten years of Crackers, with the addition of the occasional afterthought of my own or pertinent contribution or comment by somebody else. (These afterthoughts I have identified with square brackets.) But this time I have varied the formula in one respect. Ever since the enterprise started, I have made a point of never including any item that could not be fitted on to a single page. Not once have I regretted this decision, but it has left me with quite a number of otherwise potential entries which are just a little too long, and for which there has consequently been no possible outlet. In the present collection you will therefore find, as a sort of bonus at the end of each year's offering, a twenty-fifth entry not previously published. Not only does this allow me to give an airing to ten more favourite pieces that I feel have been left too long in obscurity; it also – I very much hope – gives regular readers who already possess all the annual Crackers a reason for buying this book as well.

That passing reference above to contributions by other people brings me to two important points which I emphasized in my earlier introduction but which should, I think, be repeated in this one. I am ever grateful for such contributions, and have, I trust, made proper acknowledgement for all that appear in these pages. If I have anywhere omitted to do so, I can only plead that in my excitement at the gift I must somehow have forgotten to record the name of the giver. To any benefactor still unidentified I can only offer my apologies – and my assurance that such lamentably bad manners are due to sheer absent-mindedness, rather than to any attempt to pass off their serendipity as my own.

To those who have sent me items that have not subsequently appeared, I must again stress that the annual Cracker is not, and never has been, composed of pieces culled during the previous twelve months. On the contrary, it is a selection made, nowadays in the course of a single spring weekend, from the whole accumulated corpus of the past thirty years, one or two items of which may easily have been waiting almost as long for publication. The mix is what matters; it imposes its own rules, and refuses to be hurried. If, therefore, a given contribution does not appear in the very next edition, this does not mean that it has been rejected, still less forgotten.

Inevitably, however, there remains plenty of marvellous material which, though occupying a proud and treasured place in one or another of the albums, will never find its way into a Cracker. Often the reason may be obvious enough; occasionally, on the other hand, there seems to be no rational explanation. One can only conclude that – just as characters in plays or novels tend to take on individual personalities that their creators never intended – so the Crackers too have developed, over the years and in their own infinitely more humble way, an inner logic of their own. Some pieces fit; others, of equally high quality, stubbornly refuse to settle down. Most of the latter are of my own finding; where they are not, I hope that their kind sponsors will understand, and not be discouraged from keeping up the good work.

To all those who have sent me contributions, used and unused, over the years, I am equally and eternally grateful. I must also once again record the immeasurable debts I owe to Alison Henning, without whose encouragement – described in the earlier introduction – the first Cracker might easily have been the last; to John Saumarez Smith of Messrs Heywood Hill, whose enthusiasm continues to be a moral tonic, just as his remarkable salesmanship annually provides a financial one; to my secretary, Marion Koenig, for the countless hours she spends on our increasingly difficult problems of production and distribution; and to all those, friends and strangers alike, who buy their copies year after year and so have enabled me, if not yet to hit the quarter-century, at least to come within striking distance of it – and to have high hopes for the future.

Ithaca, September 1989

A
Christmas
Cracker

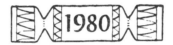

1980

Thus, in his highly entertaining book of reminiscences Time Was, *does W. Graham-Robertson describe Ellen Terry in Irving's production of* Macbeth, *December 1888:*

Her appearance was magnificent: long plaits of deep red hair fell from under a purple veil over a robe of green upon which iridescent wings of beetles glittered like emeralds, and a great wine-coloured cloak, gold embroidered, swept from her shoulders.

The effect was barbaric and exactly right, though whence the wife of an ancient Scottish chieftain obtained so many oriental beetles' wings was not explained, and I remember Oscar Wilde remarking, 'Judging from the banquet, Lady Macbeth seems an economical housekeeper and evidently patronises local industries for her husband's clothes and the servants' liveries, but she takes care to do all her own shopping in Byzantium.'

On the change of emphasis discernible in English Catholic writing since the war:

The Papists sing no longer of the hopyard and the vine,
For gall is more than Guinness is, and wormwood more than
    wine.
And Greene's too seedy café stands by Waugh's too stately
    home,
Where the rolling English drunkards made a rolling road to
    Rome.

D. A. N. Jones

The following anecdote is drawn from Toronto, No Mean City, *by my Canadian architect friend, Eric Arthur:*

. . . The city fathers decided that what Toronto needed was not a court house only, but a city hall as well and, in 1887, Lennox was asked to prepare drawings for a building to combine both functions. He did so superbly well. That it cost $2,500,000, a figure somewhat in excess of the target of $300,000 set by the City, was explained by Mayor John Shaw on opening day, 18 September 1899:

'Why people will spend large sums of money on great buildings opens up a wide field of thought. It may, however, be roughly answered that great buildings symbolize a people's deeds and aspirations. It has been said that, whenever a nation had a conscience and a mind, it recorded the evidence of its being in the highest products of this greatest of all arts. Where no such monuments are to be found, the mental and moral natures of the people have not been above the faculties of the beast.'

After such a statement from the Chief Magistrate, there were few with the temerity to put themselves on the moral level of the beasts, and question the cost of the building.

'Do not go gentle into that good night' – *it's the one line of Dylan Thomas that everybody knows. So well known is it, in fact, that I thought twice about including the poem here. But then I reflected that for every hundred people who knew the first line there was probably only one who knew the rest of it – and fewer still who realized that it was by far the best example in English of that lovely old French verse form, the Villanelle. And so, hackneyed or not, here it is:*

Do not go gentle into that good night,
Old age should burn and rave at close of day;
Rage, rage against the dying of the light.

Though wise men at their end know dark is right,
Because their words had forked no lightning they
Do not go gentle into that good night.

Good men, the last wave by, crying how bright
Their frail deeds might have danced in a green bay,
Rage, rage against the dying of the light.

Wild men who caught and sang the sun in flight,
And learn, too late, they grieved it on its way,
Do not go gentle into that good night.

Grave men, near death, who see with blinding sight
Blind eyes could blaze like meteors and be gay,
Rage, rage against the dying of the light.

And you, my father, there on the sad height,
Curse, bless, me now with your fierce tears, I pray.
Do not go gentle into that good night.
Rage, rage against the dying of the light.

In Book VII of the Iliad *Idaeus, the messenger of Zeus, separates Hector and Ajax as they fight. He, however, gives contrary advice:*

νὺξ δ' ἤδη τελέθει· ἀγαθὸν καὶ νυκτὶ πιθέσθαι.

But night is already at hand; it is well to yield to the night.

Maurice Baring used to say that, for him, it was the most beautiful line in all Homer.

I expect some people may be surprised to learn that, of all the great men and women of history whom I should most like to have known, the name of William Wilberforce comes high on the list. But listen to Sir James Stephen: in the second volume of his Essays in Ecclesiastical Biography *he writes:*

Mr Wilberforce was, by the gift of nature, among the most consummate actors of his time. Imagine David Garrick – talking not as a mime, but from the resources of his own mind, and the impulses of his own nature – to have personated in some other society the friends whom he had been dining at the Literary Club, – now uttering maxims of wisdom with Johnsonian dignity – then haranguing with a rapture like that of Burke – telling a good story with the unction of James Boswell – chuckling over a ludicrous jest with the childlike glee of Oliver Goldsmith – singing a ballad with all the taste of Percy – reciting poetry with the classical enthusiasm of Cumberland – and, at each successive change in this interlude, exhibiting the amenities of Sir Joshua – then brood awhile over this monopolylogue, and there would emerge an image of the social William Wilberforce, always the same, and ever multiform, constraining his companions to laugh, to weep, to admire, to exult, and to meditate at his bidding.

Elsewhere, Stephen is quoted reminiscing about his old friend:

'Do you remember Madame de Maintenon's exclamation? "Oh the misery of having to amuse an old King, *qui n'est pas amusable!*" Now if I were called upon to describe Wilberforce in one word, I should say he was the most "amusable" man I ever met with in my life. Instead of having to think what subjects will interest him, it is perfectly impossible to hit on one that does not. I never saw any one who touched on life at so many points; and this is the more remarkable in a man who is supposed to live absorbed in the contemplation of a future state.'

Robin Furneaux, from whose brilliant biography of Wilberforce I have lifted the above quotations, adds:

It was his reputation for saintliness and rectitude that gave the point to one of Byron's favourite stories. Sheridan, incapably drunk, was found lying in the gutter by the watch. Asked for his name the great wit raised his head and hiccuped out the words, 'William Wilberforce!' It was, in its way, a tribute.

Give me books, fruit, French wine and fine weather and a little music out of doors, played by somebody I do not know.

Keats

Unfortunate verses from well-known hymns make excellent commonplace material; they tend, however, to need a certain amount of hunting down, since most of the choicest examples have been – not altogether surprisingly – suppressed in the later editions of the hymnals. Thus it is only in the Standard Edition, and not the Revised, of Hymns Ancient and Modern *that you will find in Hymn 75 – suggested for use at the Feast of the Circumcision – the following lines:*

Lord, circumcise our hearts, we pray,
And take what is not Thine away;
Write Thine own Name upon our hearts
Thy law within our inward parts.

A footnote informs us that 'THE HYMN was written by the Abbé Besnault (†1724) and inserted in the Sens Breviary, *1726, as the Mattins Hymn for this Festival. THE TRANSLATION is based upon the version published by Chandler in his* Hymns of the Primitive Church, *1837; it has been considerably altered in this edition.' What from, one wonders, what from?*

The famous Palm Sunday hymn 'All Glory, Laud and Honour', as translated by J. M. Neale from the Latin of St Theodulph of Orleans, originally contained this verse:

Be Thou, O Lord, the Rider,
  And we the little ass,
That to God's holy city
  Together we may pass.

George Lyttelton, writing to Rupert Hart-Davis on 1 November 1956 – and what a feast is to be found in that *correspondence – quotes the last stanza of a hymn 'in use in a church near Cambridge' in the 1880s:*

Milk of the breast that cannot cloy
  He, like a nurse, will bring;
And when we see His promise nigh,
  Oh how we'll suck and sing!

Were I asked to name the worst novelist in English literature, I should unhesitatingly award the palm to Mrs Amanda McKittrick Ros. This slightly abridged extract comes from Irene Iddesleigh, *published in 1897. Sir John Dunfern has been increasingly concerned by the general surliness of his bride (who loves another) and determines on a showdown. He begins with the words 'Irene, if I may use such familiarity' – she is already heavily pregnant – and continues:*

'I, as you see, am tinged with slightly snowy tufts, the result of stifled sorrow and care concerning you alone; and on the memorable day of our alliance, as you are well aware, the black and glossy locks of glistening glory crowned my brow. There dwelt then, just six months this day, no trace of sorrow or smothered woe . . . But alas! now I feel so changed! And why?

'Because I have dastardly and doggedly been made a tool of treason in the hands of the traitoress and unworthy! . . . I was led to believe that your unbounded joy and happiness were never at such a par as when sharing them with me. Was I falsely informed of your ways and worth? Was I duped to ascend the ladder of liberty, the hill of harmony, the tree of triumph, and the rock of regard, and when wildly manifesting my act of ascension, was I to be informed of treading still in the valley of defeat?

'Speak! Irene! Wife! Woman! Do not sit in silence and allow the blood that now boils in my veins to ooze through cavities of unrestrained passion and trickle down to drench me with its crimson hue!'

Sir John continues further in this style, but Lady Dunfern can give as good as she gets:

'Sir and husband,' she said with great nervousness at first, 'you have summoned me hither to lash your rebuke unmercifully upon me, provoked, it may be, by underhand intercourse . . . You may not already be aware of the fact that I, whom you insinuate you wrested from beggary, am the only child of the late Colonel Iddesleigh, who fell a victim to a gunshot wound inflicted by the hand of his wife, who had fallen into the pit of intemperance. Yes, Earl Peden's daughter was his wife and my mother, and only that this vice so actuated her movements, I might still have lent to Society the object it dare not now claim, and thereby would have shunned the iron rule of being bound down to exist for months at a time within such a small space of the world's great bed . . .

'I now wish to retire, feeling greatly fatigued, and trusting our relations shall remain friendly and mutual, I bid thee good-night.'

The Poet Laureate,* no less, has sent me the enclosed extract from Nineteenth-Century Railway Carriages *by Hamilton Ellis (London, 1949). It comes from Chapter IV, which is entitled 'For the Very Lowest Orders'.*

The attitude of many companies was that summed up in the amiable pronouncement made by Charles Saunders, secretary of the Great Western, before a Parliamentary Committee in July 1839, that perhaps the company would arrange later on to convey the very lowest orders of passengers, once a day at very low speed in carriages of an inferior description, at a very low price, perhaps at night.

*In 1980, Sir John Betjeman.

He was one of the most luminous, eloquent blunderers with which any people was ever afflicted. For fifteen years I have found my income dwindling away under his eloquence, and regularly in every session of parliament he has charmed every classical feeling and stripped me of every guinea I possessed. At the close of every brilliant display, an expedition failed or a Kingdom fell. By the time his style had gained the summit of perfection, Europe was degraded to the lowest abyss of misery. God send us a stammerer; a tongueless man.

On Chantrey's recently-erected statue of Pitt in Hanover Square, Smith suggested the following inscription:

To the Right Honourable William Pitt
Whose Errors in Foreign Policy
And lavish Expenditure in our Resources at Home
Have laid the Foundations of National Bankruptcy
And Scattered the Seeds of Revolution
This Monument was Erected
By many weak Men, who Mistook his Eloquence for Wisdom
And his Insolence for Magnanimity
By many unworthy Men whom he had Ennobled
And by many base Men whom he had Enriched at the
Public Expense.
But for Englishmen
This Statue Raised from such Motives
Has not been Erected in vain.
They learn from it those Dreadful Abuses
Which exist under the Mockery
Of a free Representation
And feel the Deep Necessity
Of a Great and Efficient Reform.

Tempo era dal principio del mattino;
　E il sol montava in su con quelle stelle
　Ch' eran con lui, quando l'amor divino
Mosse di prima quelle cose belle.

This lovely passage from the first Canto of the Inferno *has been translated by H. F. Cary:*

The hour was morning's prime, and on his way
Aloft the sun ascended, with those stars
That with him rose when Love Divine first moved
Those its fair works . . .

I'm not too keen on that last half-line, but try as I may I can't find a better one. Strange that those three simple Italian words should be so hard to translate.

Cary's rendering of Dante, taken as a whole, still seems to me the best, even though – or perhaps because – he has stuck to safe, smooth Miltonic pentameters, avoiding the nightmare pitfalls of terza rima. *And Milton is, after all, our nearest English equivalent to Dante, despite the almost unbelievable three and a half centuries that lie between them.*

John Alexander Smith, Waynflete Professor of Moral and Metaphysical Philosophy at Oxford, began a course of lectures in 1914 with the following words:

Gentlemen, you are now about to embark upon a course of studies which will occupy you for two years. Together, they form a noble adventure. But I would like to remind you of an important point. Some of you, when you go down from the University, will go into the Church, or to the Bar, or to the House of Commons, or to the Home Civil Service, or the Indian or Colonial Services, or into various professions. Some may go into the Army, some into industry and commerce; some may become country gentlemen. A few – I hope a very few – will become teachers or dons. Let me make this clear to you. Except for those in the last category, nothing that you will learn in the course of your studies will be of the slightest possible use to you in after life – save only this – that if you work hard and intelligently you should be able to detect *when a man is talking rot*, and that, in my view, is the main, if not the sole, purpose of education.

Isaiah Berlin tells me that Professor Smith talked a good deal of rot himself. He was, however, according to the Dictionary of National Biography, *'skilful at card tricks and other forms of legerdemain' – which must surely count in his favour.*

Were I a king, I could command content;
Were I obscure, hidden should be my cares;
Or were I dead, no cares should me torment,
Nor hopes nor hates nor loves nor griefs nor fears.
A doubtful choice, of these three which to crave,
A kingdom, or a cottage, or a grave.

Edward de Vere, Earl of Oxford
(1550–1604)

In Venice, on the very tip of the Punta della Dogana, there stands a solitary lamp-post. It is made of cast iron, and on the base the legend is inscribed in bold block letters: FONDERIA DI FERRO IN VENEZIA DI THEODOR E HASSELQUIST. *This inspired John Sparrow, former Warden of All Souls, to write the following poem:*

S. MARIA DELLA SALUTE

See the Saviour Queen on high,
Crowned with stars against the sky!
Poised in her appointed place
Gravely she dispenses grace,
While, the pattern to repeat,
From the dome beneath her feet
Flows the marble, fold on fold,
Convoluted, white and cold.
Close at hand a patient pair
On their backs the planet bear;
Atlas bends beneath the strain,
Fortune flaunts her golden vane:
Lucid in the moonlight pale,
Gleams the globe and shifts the sail.

While aloft in ranks serene,
Serving their celestial queen,
Countless constellations bright
Circumnavigate the night,
Two poor earth-bound slaves below
Where the sea-fogs settle slow,
Stationed on the shadowy ledge
That defines the water's edge,
Lift their lantern through the mist –
Theodor and Hasselquist.

Air and water, sky and stone,
Need foundations not their own:
How can they subsist alone?
I, their structure to sustain,
Recompose them in my brain
Endlessly, but all in vain.
Air and water, stone and sky,
No less mortal they than I,
Human Atlas, doomed to die.

Yet there stirs within my breast
Something not to be suppressed,
Reaching out beyond my reach,
Inexpressible in speech,
Dumb presentiment of prayer
To the Queen of night and air:

> *When the globe dissolves for me*
> *And the land is lost in sea,*
> *When I cross the last lagoon*
> *Starless, and without a moon,*
> *Faithful still beneath the dome*
> *Be they there to light me home,*
> *Shining from the farther shore –*
> *Hasselquist and Theodor.*

When Mr Sparrow showed me his poem, I happened to be leaving for Venice on the following day and undertook to see what more I could find out about this mysterious pair. Alas, my researches ended in total failure – a fact which I confessed, in very small handwriting, on a postcard:

A line to say I kept my tryst
With Theodor and Hasselquist.
Just as the sun was sinking slow
Behind the Ca' Rezzonico,
I reached the lamp-post that proclaims
Those two by-now familiar names
And, running my fingers up its side,
I felt a strange, vicarious pride.
Next day I met, in Harry's Bar,
A bright encyclopaedic star
Than whom no man on earth knows more
Of Venice, and Venetian lore.
(Do call him when you're here again –
His name is Peter Lauritzen.)
He said he'd never heard before
Of Hasselquist – or Theodor –
But, when the campanile fell,
Shattering every single bell,
A firm of foreign founders settled,
Re-cast, re-clappered and re-metalled,
Till once more round San Marco rang
That same old well-remembered clang;
At which they sauntered down the wharf,
And found a ship, and buggered off.
(Although he didn't know too much
He rather thought that they were Dutch.)
But were they – still those doubts persist –
Our Theodor and Hasselquist?
Peter now rings to say he's learnt
Much to his sorrow, that they weren't.

Meanwhile, I've trudged through evening damps
Investigating all the lamps
Of Venice, which – I tell no lie –
No dog knows half so well as I.
On each I seek those names to spell;
But can I do it? Can I hell.
The monument of which we speak
'S not only lonely,* it's unique.

* You'll note, not once but several times
These sensitive internal rhymes.

Tant pis; you'd rather have, I thought,
This nil, but interim, report
Than baffled Silence. So dear John,
Take comfort: our research goes on,
And will, until we learn the score
On Hasselquist and Theodor.

[See now pp. 46–7]

In the summer of 1918, when he had less than five months left to live – he was killed, aged twenty-five, a week before Armistice Day – Wilfred Owen wrote to Osbert Sitwell from the front:

For 14 hours yesterday I was at work – teaching Christ to lift his Cross by numbers, and how to adjust his crown; and not to imagine he thirst till after the last halt; I attended his Supper to see that there were no complaints; and inspected his feet to see that they should be worthy of the nails. I see to it that he is dumb and stands to attention before his accusers. With a piece of silver I buy him every day, and with maps I make him familiar with the topography of Golgotha.

Two more pretty mnemonics for those – if such there be – who are prepared to devote a brief period of study to the task of committing to memory, in their correct chronological order, the great geological periods and the principal battles of the Wars of the Roses:

Camels Often Sit Down Carefully. Perhaps Their Joints Creak? Early Oiling Might Prevent Permanent Rheumatism.

(Cambrian, Ordovician, Silurian, Devonian, Carboniferous, Permian, Triassic, Jurassic, Cretaceous, Eocene, Oligocene, Miocene, Pliocene, Pleistocene, Recent)

A Boy Now Will Mention All The Hot, Horrid Battles Till Bosworth.

(St Albans, Blore Heath, Northampton, Wakefield, Mortimer's Cross, St Albans again, Towton, Hedgeley Moor, Hexham, Barnet, Tewkesbury, Bosworth)

After I published the above in the 1980 Cracker, my friend Betty Kilham Roberts wrote pointing out that the first mnemonic leaves out the Rhaetic period, which comes between the Triassic and the Jurassic. In her university days she preferred

Cats Of Savage Disposition Care; Perhaps, Things Relating Jungle Cats? Exceptional Orthodoxy Makes Pussies Rebel.

In all ages it hath been a favourite text that a potent love hath the nature of an isolated fatality, whereto the mind's opinions and wonted resolves are altogether alien; as, for example, Daphnis his frenzy, wherein it had little availed him to have been convinced of Heraclitus his doctrine; or the philtre-bred passion of Tristan, who, though he had been as deep as Duns Scotus, would have had his reasoning marred by that cup too much; or Romeo in his sudden taking for Juliet, wherein any objections he might have held against Ptolemy had made little difference to his discourse under the balcony. Yet all love is not such, even though potent; nay, this passion hath as large scope as any for allying itself with every operation of the soul: so that it shall acknowledge an effect from the imagined light of unproven firmaments, and have its scale set to the grander orbits of what hath been and shall be.

I would offer a small prize to anyone, coming on this passage for the first time, who correctly guessed the author. It is in fact an unattributed chapter heading from Daniel Deronda; *and I have it on no less excellent an authority than that of the editor of my Penguin edition, Professor Barbara Hardy, that it is by George Eliot herself.*

Voici les lieux charmants, où mon âme ravie
    Passait à contempler Sylvie:
Ces tranquilles moments si doucement perdus.
Que je l'aimais alors! Que je la trouvais belle!
Mon coeur, vous soupirez au nom de l'infidèle:
Avez-vous oublié que vous ne l'aimez plus?

C'est ici que souvent, errant dans les prairies,
    Ma main des fleurs les plus chéries
Lui faisait des présents si tendrement reçus.
Que je l'aimais alors! Que je la trouvais belle!
Mon coeur, vous soupirez au nom de l'infidèle:
Avez-vous oublié que vous ne l'aimez plus?

Boileau
(1636–1711)

I have often thought that much of the beauty of French as a language of poetry or – even more – of song lay in the mute 'e's, the feminine endings neither quite voiced nor quite voiceless, that allow rhythmic subtleties of which the English language knows nothing. Voltaire thought so too:

C'est précisément dans ces *e* muets que consiste la grande harmonie de notre prose et de nos vers . . . Toutes ces désinences heureuses laissent dans l'oreille un son qui subsiste encore après le mot prononcé, comme un clavecin qui résonne quand les doigts ne frappent plus les touches.

THE THEOLOGY OF BONGWI, THE BABOON

This is the wisdom of the Ape
  Who yelps beneath the Moon –
'Tis God who made me in his shape,
  He is a Great Baboon.
'Tis He who tilts the moon askew
  And fans the forest trees,
 he heavens which are broad and blue
  Provide him his trapeze,
He swings with tail divinely bent
  Around those azure bars
And munches to his Soul's content
  The kernels of the stars;
And when I die, His loving care
  Will raise me from the sod
To learn the perfect mischief there,
  The Nimbleness of God.

                  Roy Campbell

The poem opposite is inescapably reminiscent of that other brilliant evocation of a zoomorphic deity by one of its own kind – Rupert Brooke's 'Heaven:'

Fish (fly-replete, in depth of June,
Dawdling away their wat'ry noon)
Ponder deep wisdom, dark or clear,
Each secret fishy hope or fear.
Fish say, they have their Stream and Pond;
But is there anything Beyond?
This life cannot be all, they swear,
For how unpleasant, if it were!
One may not doubt that, somehow, God
Shall come of Water and of Mud;
And, sure, the reverent eye must see
A Purpose in Liquidity.
We darkly know, by Faith we cry,
The future is not Wholly Dry.
Mud unto mud! – Death eddies near –
Not here the appointed End, not here!
But somewhere, beyond Space and Time,
Is wetter water, slimier slime!
And there (they trust) there swimmeth One
Who swam ere rivers were begun,
Immense, of fishy form and mind,
Squamous, omnipotent, and kind;
And under that almighty Fin,
The littlest Fish may enter in.
Oh! never fly conceals a hook,
Fish say, in the Eternal Brook,
But more than mundane weeds are there,
And mud, celestially fair;
Fat caterpillars drift around
And Paradisal grubs are found;
Unfading moths, immortal flies,
And the worm that never dies.
And in that Heaven of all their wish
There shall be no more land, say fish.

I have never liked Versailles, but have long drawn comfort from the reflection that Horace Walpole disliked it much more than I do. He wrote to Richard West in 1739:

Stand by, clear the way, make room for the pompous appearance of Versailles le Grand! – But no: it fell so short of my idea of it, mine, that I have resigned to Gray the office of writing its panegyric. He likes it. They say I am to like it better next Sunday; when the sun is to shine, the king is to be fine, the water-works are to play, and the new Knights of the Holy Ghost are to be installed! Ever since Wednesday, the day we were there, we have done nothing but dispute about it. They say, we did not see it to advantage, that we ran through the apartments, saw the garden *en passant*, and slubbered over Trianon. I say, we saw nothing. However, we had time to see that the great front is a lumber of littleness, composed of black brick, stuck full of bad old busts, and fringed with gold rails. The rooms are all small, except the great gallery, which is noble, but totally wainscoted with looking-glass. The garden is littered with statues and fountains, each of which has its tutelary deity. In particular, the elementary god of fire solaces himself in one. In another, Enceladus, in lieu of a mountain, is overwhelmed with many waters. There are avenues of water-pots, who disport themselves much in squirting up cascadelins. In short, 'tis a garden for a great child. Such was Louis Quatorze, who is here seen in his proper colours, where he commanded in person, unassisted by his armies and generals, and left to the pursuit of his own puerile ideas of glory.

It is only fair to point out that Walpole's own taste in architecture was not universally approved by visitors from across the Channel. In 1778 the Prince de Ligne – who was something of an expert, having built several follies of his own in his garden at Beloeil – reported:

J'aime les ruines lorsqu'elles offrent une idée des choses respectables qui s'y sont passées, et des gens célèbres qui les habitaient; mais quand on voit la Grécie de plusieurs Anglais et la Gothie de Mr Walpole, on est tenté de croire que c'est le délire d'un mauvais rêve qui a conduit leur ouvrage. J'aime autant son château d'Otrant; celui de la Tamise est tout aussi fou, et n'est pas plus gai.

At St Buryan in Cornwall, on the outer wall of the south porch of the parish church, is a tablet set up by the widow of a man who died in 1795. It reads:

Sleep here Awhile
Thou Dearest part of me
In Little Time
I'll come and Sleep with Thee.

In Sir Darrell Bates's admirable Companion Guide to Devon and Cornwall, *I read that the parish church used to be a 'Royal Peculiar, Sinecure and Donative', and that the local bishop had no jurisdiction over it. Sir Darrell continues:*

The last incumbent appointed by the Crown was an aristocratic Stanhope who got the living from the Duke of York as compensation for losing a leg at the battle of Waterloo. As he had no other qualifications for the post, some difficulty was experienced in getting him ordained. In the end the following laconic letters were exchanged between the Duke and his old friend the Bishop of Cork:

Dear Cork kindly ordain Stanhope for me Yours York.

The reply came back the same day. It read:

Dear York Stanhope's ordained Yours Cork.

Stanhope drew the emoluments of the post, over a thousand a year, for 47 years without once visiting the parish, and paid his three curates £100 apiece.

George Herbert on sermons:

The worst speak something good; if all want sense,
God takes a text, and preacheth patience.

TWELFTH NIGHT
or, What Will You Have?
(Inspired by a jar of 'Old English Cocktail Olives')

Scene: The EARL OF ESSEX's *At Home.*

ESSEX: Ah, good Northumberland! Thou com'st betimes!
    What drink'st? Martini? Champagne cup? or hock?
    Or that wan distillate whose fiery soul
    Is tamed by th' hailstones hurl'd from jealous heaven,
    The draught a breed of men yet unengender'd
    Calls Scotch on th' rocks?
NORTHUMBERLAND: Ay, Scotch, but stint the rocks.
ESSEX: Ah, Gloucester! And your fairest Duchess, too!
    Sweet Leicester! Ah, my Lady Leicester, homage!
    And Worcester, and the Chesters, radiant pair!
    And Ursula, the sister of Lord Bicester!
    Northumberland, methinks thou know'st not Gloucester,
    Nor Gloucester Worcester, nor the Leicesters Chesters.
    Lord Worcester, may I introduce Lord Leicester?
    My noblest Gloucester, meet your brother Chester.
    My Lady Chester and my Lady Leicester,
    Meet Ursula, the sister of Lord Bicester.
ALL: Hail!
GLOUCESTER: Well, now, hath Phoebus quit these climes for ever?
WORCESTER: Ay, are we now delivered quite to gales,
    And spouting hurricanoes' plashy spite?
CHESTER: Sure, 'tis foul weather.
LEICESTER: Why, so 'tis.
NORTHUMBERLAND: 'Tis so.

(*Another part of the battlefield.*)

ESSEX: What ho, champagne! Crisps, ho! Pass round the peanuts!
WORCESTER: A peanut, madam? Pardon me, I pray,
    But when we met, the white-hot dazzlement
    Your beauty rains about like thunderbolts
    Quite scared my eyes; I did not catch your name.
LADY URSULA: Why, Ursula, and sister to Lord Bicester.
WORCESTER: Not Harry Bicester? Known to th' admiring world
    As Eggy? Wears a red moustache?
URSULA: The same.

WORCESTER: O, Eggy Bicester! and thou, thou art his sister?
　　Then long-lost cousins must we surely be!
ESSEX: Forgive me, Ursula, if I intrude,
　　But, Worcester, meet our brother Chester here.
　　He has the royal birthmark on his arm,
　　Would know if you had, too.
WORCESTER:　　　　　　　　Why, so I have.
CHESTER: Why, marry then, you are my brother, stol'n
　　At birth by she-bears.
WORCESTER:　　　　　　Why then, that I am!
LADY LEICESTER: The truth of th' ancient legend now is clear:
　　'When Worcester linkt to Chester prove to be,
　　Then Gloucester in Northumberland we'll see.'
　　Northumberland is Gloucester, chang'd at birth,
　　And Gloucester Worcester, while the aged Earl
　　Of Leicester plainly must be Lady Chester,
　　All chang'd, and double-chang'd, and chang'd again,
　　The Chesters Leicesters and the Leicesters Chesters,
　　Lord Chester, thus, the proof runs clear, is me,
　　And Ursula, Lord Bicester, his own sister.
NORTHUMBERLAND: Before the discourse turns again to weigh
　　Apollo's absence and the pluvious times,
　　We should acquaint our new selves with each other.
　　My Lady Chester, once the Earl of Leicester,
　　Meet Lady Leicester, now the Earl of Chester. . . .
ESSEX: Old friends 'neath curious titles oft are found,
　　Come, pass th' Old English Cocktail Olives round. . . .

Michael Frayn

A
Christmas
Cracker

1981

From an old Times Law Report:

The plaintiff, giving evidence, said that when he was on the crossing in Chertsey Street, Guildford, he heard a shout. He turned and saw the cow coming pell-mell round a corner. It trampled over him and continued on its way. He did not think it deliberately went for him.

Mr PATRICK O'CONNOR, for King Bros., submitted that the person in control of a tame animal *mansuetae naturae* – and a cow was undoubtedly tame – was not liable for damage done by it which was 'foreign to its species'. He would seek to prove the cow attacked the plaintiff; if that were so, there was no liability.

HIS LORDSHIP – Is one to abandon every vestige of common sense in approaching this matter?

COUNSEL – Yes, my Lord.

The hearing was adjourned.

Farwell, ungratefull traytor,
　　Farwell, my perjur'd swain;
Let never injur'd creature
　　Believe a man again.
The pleasure of possessing
Surpasses all expressing,
But 'tis too short a blessing
　　And love too long a pain.

'Tis easie to deceive us
　　In pity of your pain,
But when we love you leave us
　　To rail at you in vain.
Before we have descry'd it,
There is no bliss beside it,
But she that once has try'd it
　　Will never love again.

The passion you pretended
　　Was only to obtain;
But when the charm is ended
　　The charmer you disdain.
Your love by ours we measure,
Till we have lost our treasure;
But dying is a pleasure
　　When living is a pain.

I feel rather sorry to have to ascribe this sad little song to John Dryden; it comes from The Spanish Fryar, or, The Double Discovery, *where it is sung in Act V by, of all people, Leonora Queen of Arragon [sic]. One would so much prefer it to have been by Anon. – and written, perhaps, from the heart.*

From the article in the Encyclopædia Britannica (*eleventh edition*) *on the Emperor Charles V:*

Charles was undeniably plain. He confessed that he was by nature ugly, but that as artists usually painted him uglier than he was, strangers on seeing him were agreeably disappointed.

The cause of this sudden death was variously understood. By some it was ascribed to the consequences of an indigestion, occasioned either by the quantity of the wine or the quality of the mushrooms which he had swallowed in the evening. According to others, he was suffocated in his sleep by the vapour of charcoal, which extracted from the walls of the apartment the unwholesome moisture of the fresh plaster.

The second of these two possibilities is not so far-fetched as it sounds. A serious indisposition suffered by Mrs Clare Boothe Luce, United States Ambassador to Rome during the 1950s, was after thorough investigation confidently attributed to arsenic fumes emerging from the paintwork on the ceiling of her bedroom.

Regarding the Emperor Gordian, on the other hand, Gibbon has some more cheerful information:

His manners were less pure, but his character was equally amiable with that of his father. Twenty-two acknowledged concubines, and a library of sixty-two thousand volumes, attested the variety of his inclinations, and from the productions which he left behind him, it appears that the former as well as the latter were designed for use rather than ostentation.

Gibbon's own library was a good deal smaller than Gordian's – a mere six thousand volumes – and on his death it was bought as a single lot by William Beckford. Beckford's motive was a curious one: spite. Some years before, Gibbon had insulted him, and he had never forgiven the offence. Now, hearing that Gibbon had left instructions that the library should be made freely available to the public, he bought it for the sole purpose of keeping it locked up. It remained in Lausanne, and only once did he even go there to see it. Soon afterwards, he gave it away to the Swiss friend who had bought it for him. It was probably at about this time that he wrote on the endpaper of his own copy of The Decline and Fall:

> The time is not far distant, Mr Gibbon, when your almost ludicrous self-complacency, your numerous, and sometimes apparently wilful mistakes, your frequent distortion of historical Truth to provoke a jibe, or excite a sneer at everything most sacred and vulnerable, your ignorance of the oriental languages, your limited and far from acutely critical knowledge of the Latin and Greek, and in the midst of all the prurient and obscene gossip of your notes – your affected moral purity perking up every now and then from the corrupt mass like artificial roses shaken off in the dark by some Prostitute on a heap of manure, your heartless scepticism, your unclassical fondness for meretricious ornament, your tumid diction, your monotonous jingle of periods, will be still more exposed and scouted than they have been. Once fairly kicked off from your lofty, bedizened stilts, you will be reduced to your just level and true standard.   *W.B.*

The interesting thing about this diatribe is that every one of Beckford's arrows is accurately aimed. But Gibbon was still a superb writer – a hundred times greater than his attacker could ever hope to be.

[Since the publication of the 1981 Cracker, *my friend Anthony Hobson has drawn my attention to an article of his in the April 1976 number of the* Connoisseur *which rather contradicts the story told above. Having quoted Beckford's diatribe in full, he goes on:*

> In spite of this, Beckford was probably telling the truth when he said that he bought the library to read. It was rich in history and travel – both subjects that particularly interested him – and as soon as the political situation allowed, in 1802, he travelled to Lausanne, shut himself up with the books for six weeks, and read himself nearly blind.]

And talking of William Beckford, I cannot resist quoting James Lees-Milne's description of Fonthill Abbey, built by James Wyatt between 1796 and 1813, and surely the most dramatically romantic country house ever raised on English soil.

The charge so frequently levelled that Fonthill Abbey did not make a suitable residence cannot of course be gainsaid. It was preposterously, absurdly uncomfortable even in the days when indoor servants were employed by the hundred. The kitchen was seemingly miles away from the Oak Parlour where Beckford habitually dined; the eighteen bedrooms, reached by several twisted staircases of inordinate height, were practically inaccessible. Thirteen were so small, poky and lacking ventilation as to be unusable. In winter and even in summer all the rooms were as cold as tombs, so that sixty fires had to be kept burning practically throughout the year. There were no bells in the house. Instead bevies of servants were posted outside every door. There were no stables or coach-houses, only a few sheds for Beckford's carriage and ponies, for he chose to hire post horses when he travelled to London. But these and all other practical shortcomings are beside the point. Beckford was perfectly well aware of them the moment he decided to turn his folly into his home. Fonthill Abbey was intended, to quote Nikolaus Pevsner, 'to create sentiments of amazement, of shock, even of awe'. And so it succeeded. Above all it was intended to convey a scenic effect of ineffable, dream-like beauty. Like a dream it arose, and like a dream it was extinguished.

It was indeed. Less than a decade after its completion – in so far as it ever was completed – Beckford was forced to sell; and on 21 December 1825 the great tower, 276 feet high, came crashing to the ground. Today only one tiny corner survives.

And love hung still as crystal over the bed
  And filled the corners of the enormous room;
The boom of dawn that left her sleeping, showing
  The flowers mirrored in the mahogany table.

O my love, if only I were able
  To protract this hour of quiet after passion,
Not ration happiness but keep this door for ever
  Closed on the world, its own world closed within it.

But dawn's waves trouble with the bubbling minute,
  The names of books come clear upon their shelves,
The reason delves for duty and you will wake
  With a start and go on living on your own.

The first train passes and the windows groan,
  Voices will hector and your voice become
A drum in tune with theirs, which all last night
  Like sap that fingered through a hungry tree
Asserted our one night's identity.

                                    Louis MacNeice

I feel honour bound to include another extract from W. Graham-Robertson's book of reminiscences, Time Was, *if only for the opportunity it gives me to correct the ridiculous mistake I made in last year's Cracker when I called it* Time Past *[corrected in this volume]. Fortunately, it is bursting with quotable material. This story is about Holman Hunt's famous picture of the Lady of Shalott:*

The painter told me that he had always been fond of the design, yet when it was shown to Tennyson, who seemed blind and deaf to the sister arts of painting and music, the bard's only remark was: 'But I never said that her hair was flying about all over the shop like that.'

And, talking of Tennyson, here are two more stories, this time from the diary of his friend William Allingham. The scene of both is Farringford, on the Isle of Wight:

In one place are some little arches half-covered with ivy, which I pretended to believe are meant for mock ruins. This T. repudiates. He paused at a weed of goatsbeard, saying, 'It shuts up at three.' Then we went down the garden, past a large tangled fig-tree growing in the open – 'It's like a breaking wave,' says I. 'Not in the least,' says he. Such contradictions, *from him*, are noway disagreeable.

That was in 1863. Two years later, in June 1865, Allingham is at Farringford again, to find 'some people in the hayfield and Mrs [Julia Margaret] Cameron photographing everybody like mad':

Tea: enter Mrs Cameron (in a funny red open-work shawl) with two of her boys. T. appears, and Mrs C. shows a small firework toy called 'Pharaoh's Serpents', a kind of pastile which, when lighted, twists about in a worm-like shape. Mrs C. said they were poisonous and forbade us all to touch. T. in defiance put out his hand.

'Don't touch 'em!' shrieked Mrs C. 'You shan't, Alfred!' But Alfred did. 'Wash your hands then!' But Alfred wouldn't, and rubbed his moustache instead, enjoying Mrs C.'s agonies. Then she said to him: 'Will you come tomorrow and be photographed?' He, very emphatically, 'No.'

A book review from the American magazine Field and Stream, *November 1959*:

Although written many years ago, *Lady Chatterley's Lover* has just been re-issued by Grove Press, and this fictional account of the day-by-day life of an English game-keeper is still of considerable interest to outdoor-minded readers, as it contains many passages on pheasant-raising, the apprehending of poachers, ways to control vermin, and other chores and duties of the professional game-keeper.

Unfortunately, one is obliged to wade through many pages of extraneous material in order to discover and savour these sidelights on the management of a Midland shooting estate, and in this reviewer's opinion the book cannot take the place of J. R. Miller's *Practical Gamekeeper*.

Nous mangeons les fruits en silence, ce qui est toujours dans le sud un geste de rapprochement et de paix.

Dominique Fernandez
Mère Méditerranée

Here is some literary advice from Oscar Wilde. It was written to the Editor of the Pall Mall Gazette *in February 1886. The magazine had been running a series on 'The Best Hundred Books'.*

Books, I fancy, may be conveniently divided into three classes:

1. Books to read, such as Cicero's *Letters,* Suetonius, Vasari's *Lives of the Painters,* the *Autobiography of Benvenuto Cellini,* Sir John Mandeville, Marco Polo, St Simon's *Memoirs,* Mommsen, and (till we get a better one) Grote's *History of Greece.*

2. Books to re-read, such as Plato and Keats: in the sphere of poetry, the masters not the minstrels; in the sphere of philosophy, the seers not the *savants.*

3. Books not to read at all, such as Thomson's *Seasons,* Rogers's *Italy,* Paley's *Evidences,* all the Fathers except St Augustine, all John Stuart Mill except the *Essay on Liberty,* all Voltaire's plays without any exception, Butler's *Analogy,* Grant's *Aristotle,* Hume's *England,* Lewes's *History of Philosophy,* all argumentative books and all books that try to prove anything.

The third class is by far the most important. To tell people what to read is, as a rule, either useless or harmful; for the appreciation of literature is a queston of temperament not of teaching; to Parnassus there is no primer and nothing that one can learn is ever worth learning. But to tell people what not to read is a very different matter, and I venture to recommend it as a mission to the University Extension Scheme. . . .

This classification seems to me all right in theory; but what an extraordinary collection Wilde lists. I cannot believe, for example, that he got any pleasure out of Marco Polo – the most boring of all medieval travel writers, which is saying a lot. But advising people which 'classics' not to read (on artistic, not moral or political grounds, and without actually trying to stop them) – that could indeed be considered a public service.

To the memory
of
David Wall
whose superior performance
on the bassoon
endeared him
to an extensive musical
acquaintance.
His social life closed on
the 4. of December
1796
in his 57. year.

Professor Nevill Coghill died a year ago. He had taught English at Oxford for well over half a century. It is hard to give the flavour of his personality to anyone who did not know him; perhaps his letters do it best. Here is one which he wrote on 20 December 1970 to Stewart Perowne, who had asked him his views on a line in Tennyson's In Memoriam, *'I cannot understand, I love.' Stewart adds: 'My letter had quoted the well-known line from Auden in both its versions, also e.e.cummings' "Unless you love someone nothing makes any sense".'*

Dear Stewart,

Your fascinating question rings a bell but in a ruined belfry (full of bats I may add). 'We must love one another or die' wrote Wystan in his first (and preferable) version; but he has now naggingly changed it to 'We must love one another and die' so it has dwindled from an exhortation to a mere necessity. Though of course there ceases to be any force in the 'must'.

Ici on A must love B, but why should B love A?
chante B does, thank God; there is no more to say.

Ici on I rather think that somewhere behind Tennyson's thought
raconte there lies the *Credo ut intelligam* of I forgot whom. That's it, I forget every name and even Beelzebub will have to be reintroduced to me when the Time comes. If E. E. Cummings is right, then I wish someone would love *him*. I have so rarely got any sense out of him. But then I am a hopeless Square. Would I were a Park, or even a Terrace!

As for Bronwen's comment, I eagerly await your floral, oral, communication. About Sacred and Profane Love, I can tell you an Important Secret (which everybody knows): the Former becomes the Latter. Coghill's Law is slightly more complex, however, than this facile formulation. Coghill's Law is –

Ici on With Love and with Lust, I often have reckoned,
chante Whichever comes first soon turns into the second.

Readers of last year's Cracker *may remember the mystery of the lamp-post on the Punta della Dogana in Venice, with its baffling legend* FONDERIA DI FERRO IN VENEZIA DI THEODOR E HASSELQUIST. *It awoke the muse in Warden Sparrow and, more modestly, in myself; but it remains unsolved.*

Or does it? Were we both deceived by the absence of a vital full stop into thinking that there were two iron-founders responsible, when in fact there was only one? So it would appear, if we are to believe a message recently received from the Other Side through the mediumship of my friend Professor John Hale, of London University:

> I find your verse, ex-Warden Sparrow,
> Mysterious as pre-Dummett *Tarot;*
> Still worse confusions lurk, by my count,
> Within your lines, O Norwich, Viscount.
> We simple shades who mourn in Venice
> Know that your instinct with your pen is
> To double-limn or multifacet
> The plain truths of our lives. But has it
> Occurred to you that while the *city*
> Twins itself waterily (as the Gritti
> Gleams invitation to old anchors
> As well as to silk-shirted bankers),
> When you scrape your necrolatrous 'cello
> To summon up some long-dead *fellow*
> He's earned the right to gain admission
> Free from imagination's fission?
>
> Venetophiles in brassy Mailand
> Shudder to feel the past so silent!
> Find Rome's ghosts in so many layers
> They leave them to their Petrine prayers;
> Enter with joy – but leave more happily
> The glorious grottiness of Napoli.
> Lagunaphiles view with abhorrence
> Dry Calvin-cities, such as Florence;
> Prefer a mistress, proud but dirtied,
> Pearl-breasted, soignée, but damp-skirted.
> Yet damp's the seal upon our coffins,
> Trapping us for nostalgia-boffins,
> While Tuscan phantoms – who's for tennis? –
> Leap off to heaven, we're glued to Venice!
>
> Stuck cloyingly in motes of moisture
> We're forced to listen while you foist your
> Ideas of who we are upon us.
> We find you, frankly, fanfaronous.

Yes, Canophobe, and Arch-Conserver!
We've heard your mytholatory fervour!
We've read your musings turned to verses,
But now receive not *our*, MY curses!
Not Dutch! From LUND my father ventured,
But I in Brooklyn was indentured.
Then, master-foundryman, when word was
That Venice needed gas and girders,
I came here, toiled here, died here; proudly
Unpartnered, *solus*, and uncowedly,
A self-employed pyrologist.
Yours,

Theodor E. Hasselquist.

Ten years ago, in the 1971 Cracker, I quoted two of my favourite book endings. One was from Zola's La Bête Humaine. *Here is another by the same author – this time the closing paragraph of* La Fortune des Rougon:

Mais le chiffon de satin rose, passé à la boutonnière de Pierre, n'était pas la seule tache rouge dans le triomphe des Rougon. Oublié sous le lit de la pièce voisine se trouvait encore un soulier au talon sanglant. Le cierge qui brûlait auprès de M. Peirotte, de l'autre côté de la rue, saignait dans l'ombre comme une blessure ouverte. Et, au loin, au fond de l'aire Saint-Mittre, sur la pierre tombale, une mare de sang se caillait.

And how about the end of Flaubert's short story 'Hérodias', *one of the* Trois Contes? *John the Baptist (Iaokanann) has been killed, but the severed head has been recovered by three of his followers.*

Et tous les trois, ayant pris la tête de Iaokanann, s'en allèrent du côté de la Galilée.
Comme elle était très-lourde, ils la portaient alternativement.

In English, one of the best endings to any novel is that of Wuthering Heights:

I sought, and soon discovered, the three head-stones on the slope next the moor – the middle one, grey, and half buried in heath – Edgar Linton's only harmonized by the turf and moss, creeping up its foot – Heathcliff's still bare.
I lingered round them, under that benign sky; watched the moths fluttering among the heath and hare-bells; listened to the soft wind breathing through the grass; and wondered how anyone could ever imagine unquiet slumbers, for the sleepers in that quiet earth.

Charlotte Brontë wrote of her sister Emily:

Stronger than a man, simpler than a child, her nature stood alone.

Here is another splendid trouvaille *of my daughter Artemis. It is the speech made by Captain Bellamy, pirate, to Captain Beer of Boston, whose sloop he had just captured off the Carolinas. Having appropriated everything worth taking, Bellamy was in favour of returning the vessel to its owners; but his crew were determined to sink it. The text is taken from Captain Charles Johnson's* Lives of the Most Notorious Pirates, *which was published in 1724 – this incident having occurred towards the end of February 1717. Apart from its other qualities, it seems to me particularly enjoyable for being exactly the sort of language pirates were always supposed to speak; could it, perhaps, have been the prototype?*

'D—n my b—d,' says he, 'I am sorry they won't let you have your sloop again, for I scorn to do anyone a mischief, when it is not for my advantage; damn the sloop we must sink her, and she might be of use to you. Though, damn ye, you are a sneaking puppy, and so are all those who will submit to be governed by Laws which rich men have made for their own security, for the cowardly whelps have not the courage otherwise to defend what they get by their knavery. But damn ye altogether. Damn them for a pack of crazy rascals, and you, who serve them, for a parcel of hen-hearted numskulls. They villify us, the scoundrels do, when there is only this difference, they rob the poor under cover of Law, forsooth, and we plunder the rich under the protection of our own courage. Had you not better make one of us, than sneak after the a—s of those villains for Employment?'

Capt. Beer told him that his conscience would not allow him to break through the Laws of God and man.

'You are a devillish conscientious rascal, d—n ye,' replied Bellamy. 'I am a free prince, and I have as much authority to make war on the whole world as he who has a hundred sail of ships at sea, and an army of 100,000 men in the field, and this my conscience tells me. But there is no arguing with such snivelling puppies, who allow superiors to kick them about deck at pleasure and pin their faith upon a pimp of a parson, a squab, who neither practises nor believes what he puts upon the chuckle-headed fools he preaches to.'

Cassandra – the journalist William Connor – writing in the Sunday Mirror *on the funeral of Sir Winston Churchill:*

I heard no sighs. I saw no tears. This was grief exultant.

On the same subject, here are two stabbing lines from Henry VI, Part 2. *Queen Margaret is taking leave of Suffolk, who has just received his order of banishment.*

So get thee gone, that I may know my grief;
'Tis but surmised, whiles thou art standing by.

And, from Richard II*:*

You may my glories and my state depose,
But not my griefs; still am I king of those.

From the Journals of Benjamin Robert Haydon:

Carew told us a capital story of the Duke. The Duke was at the Marchioness of Downshire's, and the ladies plagued him for some of his stories. For some time he declared all his stories were in print. At last he said: 'Well, I'll tell you one that has not been printed.'

In the middle of the battle of Waterloo he saw a man in plain clothes riding about on a cob in the thickest fire. During a temporary lull the Duke beckoned him, and he rode over. He asked him who he was, and what business he had there. He replied he was an Englishman, accidentally at Brussels: that he had never seen a fight and wanted to see one. The Duke told him he was in instant danger of his life; he said 'Not more than your Grace,' and they parted. But every now and then he saw the cob-man riding about in the smoke, and at last having nobody to send to a regiment, he again beckoned to this little fellow, and told him to go up to that regiment and order them to charge – giving him some mark of authority the colonel would recognise. Away he galloped, and in a few minutes the Duke saw his order obeyed.

The Duke asked him for his card, and found in the evening, when the card fell out of his sash, that he lived at Birmingham, and was a button manufacturer! When at Birmingham the Duke enquired of the firm, and found he was their traveller, and then in Ireland. When he returned, at the Duke's request he called on him in London. The Duke was happy to see him, and said he had a vacancy in the Mint of £800 a year, where accounts were wanted. The little cob-man said it would be exactly the thing, and the Duke installed him.

My friend Christopher Gandy has called my attention to this gem from the libretto – by Francesco Maria Piave – of Verdi's opera Simon Boccanegra:

DOGE: Per me l'estrema ora suonò!

    (*Sorpresa generale*)

George Peele was a friend of Shakespeare and, more likely than not, his occasional collaborator; King Henry VI, Parts 1 *and* 3, *and* Titus Andronicus *may well be partly by his hand. He was not a very good playwright on his own; during his life he was better known as a roisterer and debauchee, and he died of the pox before he was forty. But he could, on occasion, write beautiful poetry. I quoted two short lyrics in the 1976* Cracker; *here now is something a little more ambitious. It is called 'A Farewell to Arms', and is addressed to Queen Elizabeth.*

His golden locks time hath to silver turned;
 O time too swift, O swiftness never ceasing!
His youth 'gainst time and age hath ever spurned,
 But spurned in vain; youth waneth by increasing:
Beauty, strength, youth, are flowers but fading seen;
Duty, faith, love, are roots, and ever green.

His helmet now shall make a hive for bees;
 And, lovers' sonnets turned to holy psalms,
A man-at-arms must now serve on his knees,
 And feed on prayers, which are age's alms:
But though from court to cottage he depart,
His saint is sure of his unspotted heart.

And when he saddest sits in homely cell,
 He'll teach his swains this carol for a song:
'Blest be the hearts that wish my sovereign well,
 Curst be the souls that think her any wrong.'
Goddess, allow this aged man his right,
To be your beadsman now, that was your knight.

[See now pp. 64 and 164]

Joachim du Bellay was born in 1522 and died in 1560; like Peele, he never knew old age at first hand. But perhaps in this sonnet he is not really talking about old age at all, merely that world-weariness to which youth can be every bit as subject.

Las, où est maintenant ce mépris de Fortune?
Où est ce cœur vainqueur de toute adversité,
Cet honneste désir de l'immortalité,
Et ceste honneste flamme au peuple non commune?
Où sont ces doulx plaisirs, qu'au soir sous la nuict brune
Les muses me donnoient, alors qu'en liberté
Dessus le verd tapy d'un rivage escarté
Je les menois danser aux rayons de la Lune?

Maintenant la Fortune est maistresse de moi,
Et mon cœur qui souloit estre maistre de soy
Est serf de mille maux et regrets qui m'ennuyent.
De la postérité je n'ai plus de soucy,
Cette divine ardeur, je ne l'ay plus aussi,
Et le muses de moy, comme estranges, s'enfuyent.

I once had a shot at translating it:

Alas, for where is now that scornful glance
At Fortune turned? That heart that used to bear
Ambition bright before it like a lance,
And that brave flame the others did not share?
Where are those joys the Muses would prepare
Along the river-reaches' green expanse
When, heedless in the tawny evening air,
I led them through the moonlight in a dance?

A slave: so Fortune looks upon me now –
My heart, which never master would avow,
Is plagued with vain regrets and empty dangers.
I care not what posterity may say;
That blessed fire has burnt its life away,
And all the Muses flee from me, like strangers.

I fell also to think, what advantage these innocent animals had of man, who as soon as nature cast them into the world, find their meat dressed, the cloth laid, and the table covered; they find their drink brewed, and the buttery open, their beds made, and their clothes ready; and though man hath the faculty of reason to make him a compensation for the want of those advantages, yet this reason brings with it a thousand perturbations of mind and perplexities of spirit, griping cares and anguishes of thought, which those harmless silly creatures were exempted from.

James Howell
(1594?–1666)

When Earth's last picture is painted, and the tubes are twisted
    and dried,
When the oldest colours have faded, and the youngest critic has
    died,
We shall rest, and, faith, we shall need it – lie down for an aeon
    or two,
Till the Master of all Good Workmen shall put us to work anew.

And those that were good shall be happy: they shall sit in a
    golden chair;
They shall splash at a ten-league canvas with brushes of comets'
    hair.
They shall find real saints to draw from – Magdalene, Peter
    and Paul;
They shall work for an age at a sitting and never be tired at all.

And only The Master shall praise us, and only The Master
    shall blame;
And no one shall work for money, and no one shall work for
    fame,
But each for the joy of the working, and each, in his separate star,
Shall draw the Thing as he sees It for the God of Things as
    They are!

A few years ago I used this poem by Kipling in a son et lumière *script I
wrote for Chartwell, because it perfectly reflected Churchill's own attitude
to painting. Indeed, in* Painting as a Pastime – *one of the best things he
ever wrote – he almost quoted it:*

When I get to heaven I mean to spend a considerable proportion of
my first million years in painting, and so get to the bottom of the
subject. But then I shall require a still gayer palette than I get here
below. I expect orange and vermilion will be the darkest, dullest
colours upon it and beyond them there will be a whole range of
wonderful new colours which will delight the celestial eye . . .

Elsewhere in the same book he writes:

I must say I like bright colours . . . I rejoice with the brilliant
ones, and am genuinely sorry for the poor browns.

On entre, on crie,
Et c'est la vie;
On crie, on sort,
Et c'est la mort.

Anon

I cannot vouch for the authenticity of this American publisher's letter; I can only say that it rings true to me. Perhaps some reader will be able to let me know definitively one way or the other; meanwhile, here it is.

September 8, 1961

Dear Mr Kim,

I have read the revised manuscript of THE DIVINE GOURD and on the whole I think you have done a splendid job. The ending is now very strong. As I told you, I want one or two more people to read it before coming to a final decision, but there is a more immediate problem than that. I think that Chapter XIII, when Bau makes love with Songha in the fisherman's shack, has to be entirely rewritten. I have discussed this with Elizabeth Otis and another reader here and we all agree that through a series of accidents the scene has almost the opposite effect of the one you intended because you have been rather vague about all the physical details of the scene, details which I am sure you have visualized in your mind but have not presented to the reader, so it ends up by becoming rather ludicrous.

The scene belongs in the book, and is very important in clarifying the situation . . . But it has an entirely uncharacteristic weakness: it is not visual. Throughout the rest of the book you present wonderful visual images which enable the American reader to see your Koreans and their land. Please don't misunderstand me. I am certainly not asking you to write an obscene chapter. Erotic, of course. Obscene, no. I don't know exactly how to make the distinction to you, but several of us here feel that it is more obscene to be vague than to be forthright. After all, this is the first sexual experience for both Bau and Songha, a moment of deep emotion. This has disappeared almost entirely from the scene. What are Songha's feelings? This too must be added, and it is perhaps *more important than anything else I have to suggest.* The way you handle the scene now, Songha is almost a piece of furniture.

You should be much more frank in this scene, in a pure and lyrical and idyllic way. After all, these are very young people, making love for the first time. By being vague, you simply prepare the ground for a very bad reaction from your readers, since the whole setting is very challenging. No doubt this will be the first time in literature that anyone has made love in a sardine cauldron. And for reasons too complicated to explain in a letter, please call it a *cauldron* throughout, and not a *pot.*

And this is not all. You further compound the ludicrousness of the scene by confusing two appetites – hunger and sex. It simply will not do to have Bau and Songha eat leftover sardines out of the same cauldron in which they make love. Why shouldn't there be two cauldrons, one for each appetite? Or perhaps they could find some leftover sardines elsewhere in the shack.

Another point: you have had Bau light a fire under the cauldron a little while before they begin to make love! At that point, the reader doesn't think of the idyllic moment: he worries about the blisters on Songha's bottom. I'm sorry to be so coarse about this, but these are the reactions that you arouse by vague writing. Furthermore, the fact that the shack is in darkness, and that you don't describe the banked fire very clearly, nor the kind of stove (I believe the Japanese call it a *kamado*) being used, all adds to the confusion.

It would be a great mistake to delete this scene, because it adds greatly to the structure of the book. But it must be rewritten entirely, with great care. I think you will have to provide some dim light from the fire in the shack, and give a much clearer visual description. Furthermore, you will have to prepare the reader carefully for the size of the cauldron. Unless you stress its size, the situation will seem impossible. It would help if Bau failed to light a fire under the cauldron, and if it were still kept warm by the ashes underneath. Ashes retain their heat for quite a long time. Then Songha could quite logically climb into the cauldron to keep warm, and Bau eventually, having found sardines elsewhere, could creep in to join her.

One more detail: what kind of skirt is it that is fastened around Songha's bosom? If Korean skirts do indeed fasten this way, then I think you must lay the groundwork in some detail, explaining just why Bau reached for Songha's bosom to unfasten her skirt. This is part of the general vagueness in the physical description.

I'm afraid a problem exists concerning the word *bottom*. Certainly the cauldron has a bottom, but so has Songha, and no matter how you handle your description of the cauldron, readers will inevitably associate the two bottoms. I'm afraid you had better do without the word *bottom* entirely, since there are many other words for both kinds of bottom.

I hope you will excuse me for writing in such detail. Usually language problems are not that complicated, but when it comes to sexual overtones and the free associations that go with them, the problems become unusually subtle and need careful explanation. I have spoken to Miss Otis about this . . . and we both agree that you simply have to rewrite these few pages before we take formal action on our option. Perhaps the scene should be expanded. Do you need my copy of the manuscript?

Cordially,
(Sgd.) HAROLD GREENBERG.

Was the novel ever published? And, if so, under what title? I should love to know. Or did the correspondence end with a letter beginning 'Miss Otis regrets . . .'?

A
Christmas
Cracker

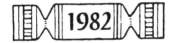

Sir Robert Baden-Powell, of Boy Scout and Mafeking fame, once wrote a book – it was first published in 1889 – called Pig-sticking or Hog-hunting; a Complete Account for Sportsmen – and Others. *On the title page there is an epigraph:*

'DUM SPIRO SPEARO' – *Old Shikari*

which must have had them in fits in the mess. I like the dedication too:

DEDICATED
by permission
to
HIS ROYAL HIGHNESS
THE
PRINCE OF WALES
who in the Pig-sticking field proved himself
in the fuller sense of the word
A Prince among Sportsmen.

On pages 204–5 of the 1924 edition there is a section entitled THE PIG HIMSELF AS AN ALLY, *in which we read:*

Among your animal allies the pig himself is perhaps your best in making the sport the sport that it is. When reading in cold blood about pig-sticking one might naturally have an underlying suspicion of the cruelty of it to the hunted animal. But after even a brief experience of the ways and nature of the pig, one becomes convinced of the fact that he alone among animals seems to enjoy being hunted ... He always seems glad to meet you and glad to die, which I cannot recall in the case of any animal of more sensitive temperament.

Last year's Cracker included 'A Farewell to Arms', by George Peele. I have since learnt from my friend John Yeoman that this was a poem of occasion, written to mark the surrender of the office of Queen's Champion, on 17 November 1590, by that redoubtable old stalwart Sir Henry Lee. Born in 1530, he is said to have watched in tears while Bishop Ridley was burnt at the stake before the gates of Balliol College, Oxford, and to have been given a new groat by him. Lee's epitaph, inscribed on a much-damaged tablet now preserved at Hartwell House, Buckinghamshire, contains the wonderful lines:

In 1611, having served five succeeding princes and kept himself right and steady in many dangerous shocks and three utter turns of state, with body bent to earth and a mind erected to heaven, aged 80, knighted 60 years, he met his long attended end.

A rather different picture of Sir Henry is given us by John Aubrey:

His dearest deare was Mris. Anne Vavasour. He erected a noble altar monument of marble whereon his effigies in armour lay; at the feet was the *Effigies* of his mistresse, Mris. Anne Vavasour. Which occasioned these verses:

> Here lies the good old Knight Sir Harry,
> Who loved well, but would not marry;
> While he lived, and had his feeling,
> She did lye, and he was kneeling,
> Now he's dead and cannot feele
> He doeth lye and she doeth kneele.

Some Bishop did threaten to have this Monument defaced; at least, to remove Mris. A. Vavasour's *effigies*.

Did the Bishop ever carry out his threat? We shall never know, just as we shall never see Sir Harry's noble monument. It stood, in its own chapel, in St Peter's church, on the edge of the little Buckinghamshire village of Quarrendon; but all that now remains of it, and of the great house where he entertained his Queen for two days in 1592, is a heap or two of stones in a meadow beside the Thames.

[Another friend, Mary Sandys, tells me that Sir Harry's portrait, and Mris. Vavasour's, hang in Armourer's Hall. The verse was apparently later set to music in the form of a catch.]

Talking of John Aubrey, here is a little-known Brief Life by that inspired parodist, the late Sir Laurence Jones – better known to those brought up on the New Statesman *competitions as 'L.E.J.' The subject is the Rev. Charles Kingsley:*

. . . He had a lean habit of body, a handsome downeright man, pale, with a greate nose, and stumbled in his speeche. He writ a sarcasticall pamphlett against Mr Newman (him that afterwards gott a red Hatt too late for his enjoyment. Quaere: was the Cardinal Manning his enemy in this?) but gott little good by it, for Mr N. (whose House had been Oriel) was too ingeniose for his downerightness and did baffle him for all he had the right in it. I have heard his brother saye 'Charles gott but a bloudy wounde for his pains.'

Scripsit . . .

Named Canon of Westminster (for which he was beholden to the Queen's Majestie) but gott no preferment being a friend to the naturall philosophie of Mr Darwin which is ill fare stomacho episcopali. He hadd greate skill to take fish with a rodd. I have seen him written downe bloudthirstie, but have forgott where.

A MADAME LULLIN

Hé, quoi! Vous êtes étonnée
Qu'au bout de quatre-vingts hivers,
Ma muse faible et surannée
Puisse encor fredonner des vers?

Un oiseau peut se faire entendre
Après la saison des beaux jours;
Mais sa voix n'a plus rien de tendre,
Il ne chante plus ses amours.

Voltaire

Lytton Strachey maintained that 'between the collapse of the Roman Empire and the Industrial Revolution three men were the intellectual masters of Europe – Bernard of Clairvaux, Erasmus and Voltaire'. I very much doubt whether either of the first two could have written as poignant a little lyric as this.

In all fairness, however, we should also record the opinion of Thomas Carlyle. To him, according to William Allingham's Diary, *Voltaire was 'a very questionable sort of article'.*

True, 'tis an unhappy circumstance of life, that Love should ever die before us; and that the Man should outlive the Lover. But say what you will, 'tis better to be left, than never to have been loved. To pass our youth in dull indifference, to refuse the sweets of life, because they once must leave us, is as preposterous, as to wish to have been born old, because we one day must be old. For my part, my youth may wear and waste, but it shall never rust in my possession.

Congreve

A similar thought occurred to Freya Stark:

I suspect anyone self-satisfied enough to refuse lawful pleasure: we are not sufficiently rich in our separate resources to reject the graces of the universe when offered; it is bad manners, like refusing to eat when invited to dinner.

There is a moment when as peaceful as the graceful impala you are still taking colour pictures. Then the sunshine is gone. A ram lifts his head. And you will feel his tension most unexpectedly in yourself. You peer up at the sky through the windscreen. Flat-bottomed clouds are turning hastily mauve, their undersides purple. The ram is standing rigid, nostrils high. A zebra shifts. Several impala cease their grazing, look about. Dark places, like some fluid spilled, are spreading where the bush grows close. Birds still rattle about. Glance up again. The clouds have turned a very dark grey in a sky from which all colour, as from a hurt man's face, is rapidly draining. Against this sky the delicate leaves of a thorn tree are becoming black lace. And without warning the buck that has been standing rigid will cross the road and with three long, high, slow-motion leaps vanish into the bush on the other side.

Now all the herds are in movement, impala and zebra alike. Panic has spread its instant message and you are not immune yourself. The herds charge past your car, zebra trotting and clambering, impala taking obstacles like winged horses in a steeplechase . . . Off in the brush the crashing of animals ceases suddenly and in the thorn tree above you birds no longer rattle. There is silence.

You try to see. You try very hard to see because night has arrived on the African continent and the importance of being able to see something has become in an instant an urgent matter. But you can see nothing. The zebras' shining rumps are out there, somewhere, but they are invisible. And so you try to hear something. You listen very hard and you find that you are holding your breath but you can hear nothing. The herd cannot be far away but it makes no sound. The birds that were your rattling companions only moments ago must still inhabit the thorn tree above you, but they give no sign. You are alone, quite alone, as each animal is alone in his pressing black silent world, each listening and waiting. And then it comes. It is a coughing sound, at first hard and slamming – then softly diminishing like an old-time steam locomotive pulling out of some distant junction. And whether or not you have ever heard the sound before, you will know that it is a lion.

Later that night at the permanent camp, where as around a native kraal a circular, continuous wall of living thorns keeps lion and leopard out of all but fancy, you will reflect. Night has visited the African continent every twenty-four hours since the world was born. And here was our Eden. How would you have survived, O Adam, without fangs or claws or motor cars, without pointed horns or leather hide, or a snout to sniff with or feet to climb with, without even petrol to camouflage your smell – how could you have survived, O most vulnerable primate, tuskless in Paradise, had you not been created with a weapon in your hand?

Robert Ardrey
African Genesis

Three opinions expressed by Dr Johnson to James Boswell.

On music:

> At Mr Macpherson's, in Sleat, he told us that he knew a drum from a trumpet, and a bagpipe from a guitar, which was about the extent of his knowledge of music. Tonight he said that if he had learnt music he should have been afraid he would have done nothing else than play. It was a method of employing the mind, without the labour of thinking at all, and with some applause from a man's self.

On cards:

> He said 'I am sorry I have not learnt to play at cards. It is very useful in life; it generates kindness and consolidates society.'

And on mourning:

> 'We must either outlive our friends or our friends outlive us; and I see no man that would hesitate about the choice.'

Lord David Cecil has pointed out that Johnson is 'an outstanding example of the charm that comes from an unexpected combination of qualities. In general, odd people are not sensible and sensible people are not odd. Johnson is both and often both at the same time.'
But he could be magnificently dotty too:

> 'Swallows certainly sleep all winter. A number of them conglobulate together, by flying round and round, and then all in a heap throw themselves under water and lie in the bed of the river.'

[Hugh Trevor-Roper protests that, dotty or not, this was merely the received opinion of the time. He bids me compare the theory about barnacle geese: 'All writers until the eighteenth century solemnly maintained that these grew on trees (attached by their beaks) from which, at a certain stage of maturity, they dropped off, like ripe plums. If they dropped off on dry land, they perished; but if on water, they swam away and became the birds we know.']

I have often reflected – and wondered why it should be – that there is nothing like a modern surname for killing a line of poetry stone dead. In the first-ever Cracker I quoted those two atrocious opening lines of Wordsworth's

Spade! with which Wilkinson hath tilled his lands

and

Clarkson! It was an obstinate hill to climb;

examples which might be followed up with a verse inspired by the Zulu War, by the understandably forgotten poet Ernest Pertwee:

Nigh twenty years have passed away
Since at Rorke's Drift, in iron mood,
'Gainst Zulu fire and assegai
That handful of our soldiers stood;
A hundred men that place to guard!
Their officers Bromhead and Chard.

I have, however, recently come upon an example more ludicrous than any of these, in which no less than nine British surnames are crammed into the pentameter of an elegiac couplet. The entry in the Dictionary of National Biography *on the Rev. Abel Evans, D.D. (1679–1737) notes that*

As an epigrammatist he had considerable reputation, and was by no means the least among the nine Oxford wits whose names are preserved in the distych –

*Alma novem genuit celebres Rhedycina poetas,
Bubb, Stubb, Cobb, Crabb, Trapp, Young, Carey, Tickell, Evans.*

'Evans' at first seemed to me difficult to pronounce iambically, with the stress on the second syllable, until I realized that the temporary adoption of a heavy Welsh accent automatically did the trick.

Sir Brian Young tells me that the third name should properly be 'Grubb'; but even he, eminent classicist as he is, cannot solve the mystery of Rhedycina. *Suggestions, please.*

[The above appeal yielded an immediate result in the form of the following lines from Jan Morris:

'Suggestions, please', the bloody Sais decreed!
But look you, Lord:
Our *ychen* laboured through that *rhyd*
Before an Ox set eyes upon the Ford.
The 'mystery' of Rhedycina, then?
Just Welsh for Oxford, boyo – *Rhydychen.]*

The French, I suspect, don't mind proper names in poetry as much as we do. Perhaps, indeed, they don't mind them at all. The second line of the following poem by Gérard de Nerval would surely have been unthinkable in English; in French, it hardly seems to matter. Anyway, I find the rest of the poem so haunting that I shall quote it in full:

Il est un air pour qui je donnerais
Tout Rossini, tout Mozart et tout Weber;
Un air très vieux, languissant et funèbre,
Qui pour moi seul a des charmes secrets.

Or, chaque fois que je viens à l'entendre,
De deux cents ans mon âme rajeunit: –
C'est sous Louis treize; et je crois voir s'étendre
Un coteau vert, que le couchant jaunit.

Puis un château de brique à coins de pierre,
Aux vitraux teints de rougeâtres couleurs,
Ceint de grands parcs, avec une rivière
Baignant ses pieds, qui coule entre des fleurs;

Puis une dame, à sa haute fenêtre,
Blonde aux yeux noirs, en ses habits anciens,
Que, dans une autre existence, peut-être,
J'ai déjà vue, . . . – et dont je me souviens!

There is also a poem, arguably less successful, by Paul Eluard entitled 'Les Gertrude Hoffmann Girls', of which the first verse runs:

Gertrude, Dorothy, Mary, Claire, Alberta,
Charlotte, Dorothy, Ruth, Catherine, Emma,
Louise, Margaret, Ferral, Harriet, Sara,
Florence toute nue, Margaret, Toots, Thelma . . .

It's almost worth it for Toots.

Thou art so true that thoughts of thee suffice
To make dreams truths and fables histories.

John Donne

Ten years ago, in the 1972 Cracker, *I quoted what seemed to me a remarkably sinister letter from the author of* Alice's Adventures in Wonderland *to a little girl, enclosing the gift of a penknife. I now discover that she was not the only recipient of such things: my friend Professor Robert Martin, now in far Hawaii, has called my attention to another letter, written less than a year later, to Hallam Tennyson, son of the poet.*

Ch. Ch. Oxford
Jan. 23. 1862.

My dear Hallam,

Thank you for your nice little note. I am glad you liked the knife, and I think it a pity you should not be allowed to use it 'till you are older'. However, as you *are* older now, perhaps you have begun to use it by this time: if you were allowed to cut your finger with it, once a week, just a little, you know, till it began to bleed, and a good deep cut every birthday, I should think that would be enough, and it would last a long time so. Only I hope that if Lionel ever wants to have *his* fingers cut with it, you will be kind to your brother, and hurt him as much as he likes.

If you will send one word, some day, when your two birthdays are, perhaps I may send *him* a birthday present, if I can only find something that will hurt him as much as your knife: perhaps a blister, or a leech, or something of the sort.

Give him half my love, and take the rest yourself.

Your affectionate friend,
Charles L. Dodgson.

I know little Spanish; but one does not have to be bilingual to feel the power and beauty of two stabbing lines by Francisco Quevedo:

Su tumba son de Flándes las campañas
Y su epitafio la sangrienta luna.

The fields of Flanders are his sepulchre
And all his epitaph, the bloodshot moon.

Quevedo lived from 1580 to 1645, was secretary to Philip IV, but spent the closing years of his life in prison for his opposition to the policies of the Duke of Olivares. The lines are quoted by Maurice Baring – though he translates them a little differently – in his superb anthology Have You Anything To Declare? *He naturally adds that Flanders' fields 'have a special message for many English men and women' – the book was published in 1936 – but omits to point out that for Quevedo and his generation that message was just as poignant, and in much the same way.*

In the 1975 Cracker I included an item from an old Who's Who, *and was rewarded by a fascinating follow-up letter from a lady who had known – and indeed narrowly escaped being murdered by – its subject in later life. (Her story will be found in* Christmas Crackers, *1970–1979, pp. 150–1.) I can hardly hope for such a piece of luck again, particularly since Mrs Emily Crawford died nearly seventy years ago, on 30 December 1915; but you never know . . .*

CRAWFORD, Mrs Emily, Paris Correspondent of *Daily News*, 1885–1907; *b.* Dublin; descended on paternal side from an old Scotch Dumfriesshire family: on maternal from Merydiths of Shrewland, Co. Kildare, Eustaces of Castlemore, Co. Carlow, Martins of Connemara: *d.* of Robert Andrew Johnstone and Grace Anne Martin: *m.* George Morland Crawford, Chelsfield Court, Kent, barrister-at-law, Lincoln's Inn, and Paris Correspondent, *Daily News*, 1851–85; two *s. Educ.:* home. *Publications: Victoria, Queen and Ruler,* 1903: History day-by-day or week-by-week in different journals, but chiefly in *Daily News, Truth* and *New York Tribune:* has written much under pseudonyms; however, history thus written is like snow falling on the sea. *Recreations:* a quiet rubber of whist; hardly ever knows what tedium is; is a constantly interested observer of animated nature; has found real life so interesting that novels and plays seem flat; roughed it in the war of 1870 and during the Commune, and feels thankful for the education thus acquired. Was offered by President Carnot the decoration of the Legion of Honour; has known most of the great authors, artists, statesmen, and public speakers of her time. *Address:* Boul. de Courcelles 60, Paris.

Paradise Lost – *how could I have waited fifty-two years to read it from end to end? Here are the first three passages I marked; one from each of the first three Books:*

Jehovah, who in one night when he pass'd
From Egypt marching, equal'd with one stroke
Both her first born and all her bleating Gods.

Book I

                    . . . thir fatall hands
No second stroke intend, and such a frown
Each cast at th' other, as when two black Clouds
With Heav'n's Artillery fraught, come rattling on
Over the Caspian, then stand front to front
Hov'ring a space, till Winds the signal blow
To joyn thir dark Encounter in mid air.

Book II

Fountain of Light, thyself invisible
Amidst the glorious brightness where thou sit'st
Thron'd inaccessible, but when thou shad'st
The full blaze of thy beams, and through a cloud
Drawn round about thee like a radiant Shrine,
Dark with excessive bright thy skirts appeer,
Yet dazle Heav'n, that brightest Seraphim
Approach not, but with both wings veil their eyes.

Book III

And, in Book IV, that magical single line

Imparadis't in one another's arms.

And here are some thoughts about Paradise Lost, *as confided by Virginia Woolf to her diary on 10 September 1918:*

I am struck by the extreme difference between this poem and any other. It lies, I think, in the sublime aloofness and impersonality of the emotions ... The substance of Milton is all made of wonderful, beautiful, and masterly descriptions of angels' bodies, battles, flights, dwelling-places. He deals in horror and immensity and squalor and sublimity, but never in the passions of the human heart. Has any great poem ever let in so little light upon one's own joys and sorrows? I get no help in judging life; I scarcely feel that Milton lived or knew men and women; except for the peevish personalities about marriage and the woman's duties. He was the first of the masculinists; but his disparagement rises from his own ill luck, and seems even a spiteful last word in his domestic quarrels. But how smooth, strong and elaborate it all is! What poetry! I can conceive that even Shakespeare after this would seem a little troubled, personal, hot and imperfect. I can conceive that this is the essence, of which almost all other poetry is the dilution. The inexpressible fineness of the style, in which shade after shade is perceptible, would alone keep one gazing in to, long after the surface business in progress has been despatched. Deep down one catches still further combinations, rejections, felicities and masteries. Moreover, though there is nothing like Lady Macbeth's terror or Hamlet's cry, no pity or sympathy or intuition, the figures are majestic; in them is summed up much of what men thought of our place in the universe, of our duty to God, our religion.

During the momentous events of the early summer [the Falklands war] the words of Nelson's matchless prayer, written in his cabin on the morning of Trafalgar, kept returning to my mind. They still do.

May the Great God, whom I worship, grant to my country, and for the benefit of Europe in general, a great and glorious victory; and may no misconduct in any one tarnish it; and may humanity after victory be the predominant feature in the British Fleet. For myself, individually, I commit my life to Him who made me, and may His blessing light upon my endeavours for serving my country faithfully. To Him I resign myself and the just cause which is entrusted to me to defend. Amen. Amen. Amen.

From Sidney Hutchison's fascinating History of the Royal Academy, 1768–1968, *I was relieved to learn that in 1893 the Academy finally yielded to mounting pressure from its female students to be allowed a male nude model. The ensuing decree, however, made it clear that proper standards of decency were still to be upheld:*

> It shall be optional for Visitors in the Painting School to set the male model undraped, except about the loins, to the class of Female Students. The drapery to be worn by the model to consist of ordinary bathing drawers, and a cloth of light material 9 feet long by 3 feet wide, which shall be wound round the loins over the drawers, passed between the legs and tucked in over the waist-band; and finally a thin leather strap shall be fastened round the loins in order to insure that the cloth keep its place.

If, though, any of my readers should determine, according to their means, to set themselves to the revival of a healthy school of architecture in England, and wish to know in few words how this may be done, the answer is clear and simple. First, let us cast out utterly whatever is connected with the Greek, Roman or Renaissance architecture, in principle or in form. The whole mass of the architecture, founded on Greek and Roman models, which we have been in the habit of building for the last three centuries is utterly devoid of all life, virtue, honourableness, or power of doing good. It is base, unnatural, unfruitful, unenjoyable, and impious. Pagan in its origin, proud and unholy in its revival, paralysed in its old age, yet making prey in its dotage of all the good and living things that were springing around it in their youth, as the dying and desperate king, who had long fenced himself so strongly with the towers of it, is said to have filled his failing veins with the blood of children;* an architecture invented, as it seems, to make plagiarists of its architects, slaves of its workmen, and sybarites of its inhabitants; an architecture in which intellect is idle, invention impossible, but in which all luxury is gratified, and all insolence fortified; – the first thing we have to do is to cast it out, and shake the dust of it from our feet for ever.

Ruskin
The Stones of Venice

* Louis XI. 'In the month of March, 1481, Louis was seized with a fit of apoplexy at St. Benoît-du-lac-mort, near Chinon. He remained speechless and bereft of reason three days; and then, but very imperfectly restored, he languished in a miserable state. . . . "To cure him", says a contemporary historian, "wonderful and terrible medicines were compounded. It was reported among the people that his physicians opened the veins of little children, and made him drink their blood, to correct the poorness of his own."' (Bussey's *History of France*, London, 1850)

Walking, walking, I plod endlessly
Along the road that leads me away from you.
More than ten thousand *li* separate us,
For you and for me, the horizon is otherwise.
Long and laborious are the routes,
Nor are we sure of seeing each other again.
The Mongolian horses are harnessed to the North Wind.
Birds from the land of Hiu are perched on the branches of the
    South.

And I am leaving you,
My robes billowing out more fully from my body.
The drifting clouds veil the sun,
The voyager will never again return.
I age rapidly thinking of you;
Months and years have already flitted away.
But say no longer that we are abandoned.
Let us merely try, you and I, to eat more heartily.

Anon., Han dynasty
(206 BC–AD 220)

Elle était nue avec un abandon sublime
Et, couchée en un lit, semblait sur une cime.
A mesure qu'en elle entrait l'amour vainqueur
On eût dit que le ciel lui jaillissait du coeur;
Elle vous caressait avec de la lumière;
La nudité des pieds fait la marche plus fière
Chez ces êtres pétris d'idéale beauté;
Il lui venait dans l'ombre au front une clarté
Pareille à la nocturne auréole des pôles;
A travers les baisers, de ses blanches épaules
On croyait voir sortir deux ailes lentement;
Son regard était bleu, d'un bleu de firmament;
Et c'était la grandeur de cette femme étrange
Qu'en cessant d'être vierge elle devenait ange.

Victor Hugo
Toute la Lyre

My goddaughter Allegra Huston tells me that every passenger arriving at the airport of Guadalajara, Mexico, is handed a little booklet of local information; she has kindly brought me back a copy. It is printed in Spanish on the left-hand page and – theoretically – in English on the right. British and American travellers will find the left-hand page more useful.

The right-hand page, however, is not without its charm. Take, for example, the section entitled 'Emergency Medical Service':

> In the ground floor on the offices section, it has a consultin room and emergency medical service open from 7:00 a.m. to 11:00 p.m. in which they will provide you a unique attention, specially those cases of: traumatism digestives, changes of artery pressure, respiratory, neurotics, gynecology, endocrimology, etc.

Another section, 'To Leave the Country,' warns you that

> If you have less than 18 years old, you must go with our parents or have a notarized letter permission from your accompanist.

Best of all, however, is the opening section, 'Welcome to Guadalajara':

> ... It is ubicated 1,532 meters over sea level and counts with an annual average climate of 22 degrees. ... This state count with 124 towns. Each town is govern by a municipal president and his council.
>
> His principal symbol, is his catedral – with its qualities towers and as Pepe Guizar (a Mexican musical painter borned here) would say in his famous and popular song called Guadalajara: 'Are his Cathedral towers as backstroke plants.'

When I reproduced the diabolically difficult 'Dictée de Mérimée' in 1974, everybody pointed out that French dictations were, of course, a great deal harder than English ones. So they are; but while Philip Ziegler was researching his biography of my mother, the late Sir Alan Lascelles gave him a copy of an English dictation which, he claimed, was concocted and tried out at Belvoir Castle before the First World War. Arthur Balfour is said to have made fourteen mistakes, Raymond Asquith ten. Alternative admissible spellings are given in brackets.

The most skilful gauger was a malignant cobbler, possessing a poignant disposition, who drove a pedlar's wagon (waggon), using a goad as an instrument of coercion to tyrannise (-ize) over his pony. He was a Galilean and Sadducee, and suffered from phthisical diphtheria and a bilious intermittent erysipelas. A certain sibyl with the sobriquet (soubriquet) of a gipsy (gypsy) went into ecstasy at seeing him measure some peeled potatoes and saccharine tomatoes with dyeing and singeing ignitable (-ible) materials.

On becoming paralysed with haemorrhage, lifting her eyes to the ceiling of the cupola to conceal her unparalleled embarrassment, she made a rough curtsey (curtsy), and not harassing him with mystifying, rarefying innuendoes, she gave him for a couch a bouquet of lilies, mignonette, fuchsias, chrysanthemums, dahlias, a treatise on pneumonia, a copy of the Apocrypha in hieroglyphics, a daguerreotype of Mendelssohn, a kaleidoscope, a drachm (dram) of ipecacuanha, a teaspoonful of naphtha for delible purposes, a clarinet, some liquorice, a cornelian of symmetrical proportions, a chronometer with movable (moveable) balance, a box of loose dominoes and a catechism. The gauger was a trafficking parishioner who preferred the Pentateuch. His choice was reparable, vacillating, and with occasionally recurring idiosyncrasies. He woefully uttered an apothegm (apophthegm): 'Life is chequered, but schism, apostasy, heresy and villainy must be punished.' The sibyl, apologising (-izing), answered: 'There is ratably (rateably) an eligible choice between an ellipsis and a trisyllable.'

*An American literary agent now living in London has, I understand,
recently received the following letter from a San Francisco priest:*

Perhaps you have heard of me and my nationwide campaign in
the cause of temperance. Each year, for the past fourteen years, I
have made a tour of Northern California and delivered a series of
lectures on the evils of Drinking.

On these tours, I have been accompanied by my young friend
and assistant, Clyde Lindstrom. Clyde, a young man of good
family and excellent background, is a pathetic case whose life was
ruined by excessive indulgence in whiskey, gambling, and
women.

Clyde would appear with me at lectures and sit on the platform
wheezing and staring at the audience through bleary, bloodshot
eyes while I would point him out as an example of what drinking
would do to a person.

Last summer, unfortunately, Clyde died. A mutual friend has
given me your name, and I wonder whether you would care to
take Clyde's place on my spring tour.

Yours sincerely,
(The Rev.) Joseph D. Citarella.

Last year I was asked to be the reader/narrator/compère of the annual series of Christmas Carol Concerts given by the Royal Liverpool Philharmonic Society. This involved a most enjoyable search for about a dozen bits of suitably seasonal but unhackneyed material – during which I came across the following. It is by the American poet Phyllis McGinley:

ALL THE DAYS OF CHRISTMAS

What shall my true love
Have from me
To pleasure his Christmas
Wealthily?
The partridge has flown
From our pear tree.
Flown with our summers
Are the swans and the geese.
Milkmaids and drummers
Would leave him little peace.
I've no gold ring
And no turtle dove,
So what can I bring
To my true love?

A coat for the drizzle
Chosen at the store;
A saw and a chisel
For mending the door;
A pair of red slippers
To slip on his feet;
Three striped neckties;
Something sweet.

He shall have all
I can best afford –
No pipers piping,
No leaping lord,
But a fine fat hen
For his Christmas board;
Two pretty daughters
(Versed in the role)
To be worn like pinks
In his buttonhole;
And the tree of my heart
With its calling linnet –
My evergreen heart
And the bright bird in it.

Here is a correspondence discovered – in a remarkable state of preservation – by Maurice Baring at Mycenae, and later published by him in his book Dead Letters*:*

Clytaemnestra to Aegisthus

Mycenae

Honoured Sir,

I am sorry I was out when you came yesterday. I never thought that you seriously meant to come. I shall be very busy all next week, as Helen and Menelaus are arriving and I must get everything ready. Orestes was quite delighted with the cup and ball. You spoil him.

Yours sincerely,
Clytaemnestra.

Clytaemnestra to Aegisthus

Most honoured Aegisthus,

One line to say that I have received your letter and *loved* it all except the last sentence. Please do not say that kind of thing again as it will quite ruin our friendship, which I thought was going to be so *real*.

Yours very sincerely,
Clytaemnestra.

Clytaemnestra to Aegisthus

Most honoured Aegisthus,

The flowers are beautiful, and it was kind of you to remember my birthday. But your letter is really too naughty. . .

(The rest of this letter is missing)

Clytaemnestra to Aegisthus

Most honoured Sir,

This is to say that since you persist in misunderstanding me and refuse to listen to what I say, our correspondence must end. It is extraordinary to me that you should wish to debase what might have been so great and so wonderful.

Yours truly,
Clytaemnestra

Clytaemnestra to Aegisthus

Most honoured Aegisthus,

I was much touched by your letter and I will give you the one more trial you ask for so humbly and so touchingly.

Paris has arrived. I don't know if you know him. He is the second son of the King of Troy. He made an unfortunate marriage with a girl called Œnone, the daughter of a rather disreputable river-person. They were miserable about it. He is very good-looking – if one admires those kind of looks, which I don't. He dresses in an absurd way and he looks theatrical. Besides, I hate men with curly hair. He has a few accomplishments. He shoots well and plays on the double flute quite remarkably well for a man who is not a professional; but he is totally uninteresting, and, what is more, impossible. But Helen likes him. Isn't it extraordinary that she always has liked impossible men? They sit for hours together saying nothing at all. I don't in the least mind his paying no attention to me – in fact, I am too thankful not to have to talk to him; but I do think it's bad manners, as I am his hostess.

Helen is certainly looking better this year than she has ever looked; but she still dresses in that affectedly over-simple way, which is a pity. I don't know how long he is going to stay. I don't mind his being here, but Helen and he are really most inconsiderate. They use my sitting-room as though it were theirs, and they never seem to think that I may have things to do of my own, and they expect me to go out with them, which ends in their walking on ahead and my being left with Menelaus, whom I am very fond of indeed, but who bores me. He talks of nothing but horses and quoits. It is a great lesson to Queen Hecuba for having brought up her son so badly. Paris was educated entirely by a shepherd, you know, on Mount Ida. The result is his manners are shocking. Helen doesn't see it. Isn't it odd? I must say he's nice with children, and Orestes likes him.

I am your sincere friend,
Clytaemnestra.

Clytaemnestra to Aegisthus

Mycenae

Most honoured Aegisthus,

We are in great trouble. I told you Helen was attracted by

Paris. We of course thought nothing of it, because Helen always has flirted with rather vulgar men, and her flirtations were, we thought, the harmless distractions of a woman who has remained, and always will remain, a sentimental girl.

Imagine our surprise and dismay! Paris and Helen have run away together, and they have gone to Troy! Helen left a note behind for Menelaus saying she realized that she had made a mistake, that she hated hypocrisy, and thought it more honest to leave him. She said she would always think of him with affection. Poor Menelaus is distracted, but he is behaving beautifully.

Agamemnon is furious. He is overcome by the disgrace to his family, and he is so cross. We are all very miserable. Agamemnon says that the family honour must be redeemed at all costs, and that they will have to make an expedition against Troy to fetch Helen back. I think this is quite ridiculous. No amount of expeditions and wars can undo what has been done. I am sure you will sympathize with us in our trouble. I must say it is most unfair on my children. I shouldn't have minded so much if Iphigenia wasn't grown up.

Electra has got whooping-cough, but she is going on as well as can be expected. I have no patience with Helen. She always was utterly thoughtless.

Your sincere friend,
Clytaemnestra.

Clytaemnestra to Aegisthus

Mycenae

Most honoured Aegisthus,

There is no end of worry and fuss going on. Odysseus, the King of Ithaca, has arrived here with his wife, Penelope. They discuss the prospects of the expedition from morning till night, and I am left alone with Penelope. She has borrowed my only embroidery frame, and is working some slippers for her husband. They are at least two sizes too small. She talks of nothing but her boy, her dog, her diary, and her garden, and I can't tell you how weary I am of it. She made me very angry yesterday by saying that I spoilt Orestes, and that I should be sorry for it some day. She is always throwing up her boy Telemachus to me. Whenever Helen is mentioned she puts on a face as much as to say: 'Do not defile me.'

Your sincere friend,
Clytaemnestra.

Clytaemnestra to Aegisthus

Mycenae

Most honoured Aegisthus,

My worst fears have been realized. They are going to make an expedition against Troy on a large scale. Odysseus is at the bottom of it. I cannot say how much I dislike him. All the Kings have volunteered to go, but the Fleet will not be ready for two years, so I am in hopes that something may happen in the meantime to prevent it.

Iphigenia is learning to make bandages, and says she will go to the front to look after the wounded. I am, of course, against this, and think it's absurd, but unfortunately she can make her father do what she likes. My only consolation is that the war cannot possibly last more than a week. The Trojans have no regular army, they are a handful of untrained farmers, and the town cannot stand a siege. It is all too silly. It is too bad of Helen to have caused all this fuss.

Your sincere friend,
Clytaemnestra.

P.S. – No, of course I haven't written to Helen. She is as good as dead to me.

Clytaemnestra to Aegisthus (*Two years later*)

Mycenae

My dear Aegisthus,

We have at last got some news. The Fleet has arrived at Aulis, and they are waiting for a favourable wind to be able to go on. At present they are becalmed. They are all well. Iphigenia writes that she is enjoying herself immensely. She has the decency to add that she misses me. I have not had a good night's rest since they have started.

Your most sincere friend,
Clytaemnestra.

Clytaemnestra to Aegisthus

My dear friend,

Please come here at once. I am in dreadful trouble. From the last letter I received from Agamemnon I understood there was something wrong and that he was hiding something. Today I got a letter from Calchas, breaking to me in the most brutal manner an appalling tragedy and a savage, horrible, and impious crime! They have sacrificed my darling Iphigenia – to Artemis, of all goddesses! – to get a propitious wind for their horrible Fleet! I am heartbroken. I cannot write another word. Please come directly.

Your friend,
Clytaemnestra.

Clytaemnestra to Aegisthus (*Two months later*)

I see no reason why you should not come back; I have a right to ask whom I like to stay here. Do come as soon as possible; I am very lonely without you. Now that I no longer communicate with Agamemnon in order to get news I have written to Helen and sent the letter by a very clever silk merchant, who is certain to be able to worm his way into Troy. Come as soon as you get this.

C.

P.S. – Agamemnon still writes, but I do not take the slightest notice of his letters. I trust the Trojans will be victorious. They have at any rate determined to make a fight for it. Our generals are certain to quarrel, Achilles and Agamemnon never get on well. And Achilles' temper is dreadful.

Clytaemnestra to Aegisthus (*Three months later*)

I can no longer bear these short visits and these long absences. I have arranged for you to stay here permanently.

I wrote to Agamemnon last month a cold and dignified business letter, in which I pointed out that unless some man came here to look after things, everything would go to pieces. I suggested you. I have now got his answer. He agrees, and thinks it an excellent plan.

Odysseus wrote me, I must say, a most amusing letter. He says everything is at sixes and sevens, and that Priam's eldest son is far the most capable soldier on either side. He expects to win, but says it will be a far longer business than they thought it would be at first. Come as quickly as you can. Best and most beloved.

Your C.

Helen to Clytaemnestra (Ten years later)

Dearest Clytaemnestra,

Your letters are a great comfort to me when I get them, which
is very seldom. Everything is going on just the same. It is now the
tenth year of the siege, and I see no reason why it should ever
end. I am dreadfully afraid the Greeks will never take Troy.

I can give you no idea of how dull everything is here. We do
the same thing and see the same people every day. We know
exactly what is going on in the Greek camp, and most of the time
is spent in discussing the gossip, which bores me to death. You
are quite right in what you say about Paris. I made a fatal
mistake. It is all Aphrodite's fault. He has become too dreadful
now. He is still very good-looking, but even compared with
Menelaus he is pitiable in every way and every bit as cross.
Hector is very nice, but painfully dull. The King and the Queen
are both very kind, but as for Cassandra, she is intolerable. She is
always prophesying dreadful calamities which never come off.
She said, for instance, that I would lose my looks and make a long
journey to Egypt. As if I would go to Egypt from here! As to my
looks, you know, darling, I never was vain, was I? But I can
honestly tell you that, if anything, I have rather *improved* than
otherwise, and among the Trojans' women, who are absolute
frights and have no more idea of dressing than sheep, I look
magnificent. Andromache has got quite a nice face, and I really
like her; but you should see her figure – it's like an elephant's,
and her feet are enormous, and her hands red and sore from
needlework. She won't even use a thimble! Cassandra always
dresses in deep mourning. Why, we cannot conceive, because none
of her relatives have been killed.

There is really only one person in this palace I can talk to –
and that is Aeneas, who is one of the commanders. He is quite
nice. What I specially like about him is the nice way in which he
talks about his parents.

The Greeks are quarrelling more than ever. Achilles won't
fight at all because Agamemnon insisted on taking away Briseis
(who is lovely) from him. Wasn't that exactly like Agamemnon?
I hope this won't make you jealous, darling, but I don't
expect it will, because you have never forgiven Agamemnon, have
you?

Everybody tries to be kind to me, and I have nothing to
complain of. They all mean well, and in a way this makes it
worse. For instance, every morning, when we meet for the
midday meal, Priam comes into the room saying to me: 'Well,

how's the little runaway today?' He has made this joke every day for the last ten years. And then they always talk about the cowardice and incompetence of the Greeks, taking for granted that as I have married into a Trojan family I must have become a Trojan myself. It is most tactless of them not to understand what I must be feeling.

I suppose I am inconsistent, but the pro-Greek party irritate me still more. They are headed by Pandarus, and are simply longing for their own side to be beaten, because they say that I ought to have been given up directly, and that the war was brought about entirely owing to Priam having got into the hands of the Egyptian merchants.

I managed to get some Greek stuffs smuggled into the town, and the merchants tell me vaguely what people are wearing at Mycenae; but one can't get anything properly made here. Andromache has all her clothes made at home by her women – to save expense. She says that in times of war one ought to sacrifice oneself. Of course, I can't do this, however much I should like to, as the Trojans expect me to look nice, and would be very angry if I wasn't properly dressed.

I feel if I could only meet Odysseus we might arrange some plan for getting the Greeks into the town.

How is everything going on at home? There is a very strict censorship about letters, and we are all supposed to show our letters to Antenor before they go. I don't, of course. I daresay, however, many of your letters have been intercepted, because I have only heard from you five times since the siege began, and not once this year. Kiss the dear children from me.

Shall I ever see you again? I shall try my best to come home.

Your loving sister,
Helen.

Clytaemnestra to Helen

Mycenae

Dearest Helen,

Your last letter has reached me. I must implore you to be very careful about what you do. I hope with all my heart that the siege will be over soon; but if it is I don't think it would be quite wise for you to come back directly. You see everybody here is extremely unreasonable. Instead of understanding that Agamemnon and Odysseus were entirely responsible for this absurd war, Agamemnon has got his friends to put the blame entirely on you, and they have excited the people against you. It's so like a man, that, isn't it? I have been very lonely, because all our friends are away. Aegisthus is staying here just to look after the household and the affairs of the city. But he hardly counts, and he is so busy that I hardly ever see him now. There is a strong pro-Trojan party here, too. They say we had absolutely no right to go to war, and that it was simply an expedition of pirates and freebooters, and I must say it is very difficult to disprove it. If there is any talk of the siege ending, please let me know *at once*. Electra has grown into a fine girl; but she is not as lovely as poor darling Iphigenia.

Your loving sister,
Clytaemnestra.

Penelope to Odysseus

Ithaca

My darling Husband,

I wish you would write a little more distinctly; we have the greatest difficulty in reading your letters.

When will this horrid siege be over? I think it is disgraceful of you all to be so long about it. To think that when you started you only said that it would last a month! Mind you come back the moment it is over, and come back *straight*, by Aulis.

The country is looking lovely. I have built a new house for the swineherd, as he complained about the roof letting the rain in. Next year, we must really have a new paling round the garden, as the children get in and steal the apples. We can't afford it *this* year. The people have no sense of honesty; they steal everything. Telemachus is very well. He can read and write nicely, but is most backward about his sums. He takes a great interest in the war, and has made up a map on which he marks the position of the troops with little flags.

I am surprised to hear of Achilles' *disgraceful* conduct. If I were there I would give him a piece of my mind. I hope Ajax has not had any more of his attacks. Has he tried cinnamon with fomented myrtle leaves? It ought to be taken three time a day *after* meals. The news from Mycenae is deplorable. Clytaemnestra appears to be quite shameless and callous. Aegisthus is now openly living in the house. All decent people have ceased to go near them. I have had a few visitors, but nobody of any importance.

I am working you a piece of tapestry for your bedroom. I hope to get it finished by the time you come back. I hope that when the city is taken Helen will be severely punished.

We have taught Argus to growl whenever Hector is mentioned. I don't, of course, allow any one to mention Helen in this house.

Telemachus sends you his loving duty. He is writing to you himself, but the letter isn't finished.

Your devoted wife,
Penelope.

Helen to Clytaemnestra

Sunium

Dearest Clytaemnestra,

Since I last wrote to you several important things have happened. Hector was killed yesterday by Achilles. I am, of course, very sorry for them all. All Cassandra said was, 'I told you so!' She is so heartless. I have at last managed to communicate with Odysseus; we have thought of a very good plan for letting the Greeks into the city. Please do not repeat this. I shall come home at once with Menelaus. He is my husband, after all. I shall come straight to Mycenae. I doubt if I shall have time to write again. I am sending this through Aenida, who is most useful in getting letters brought and sent.

Please have some patterns for me to choose from. I hope to be back in a month.

Your loving sister,
Helen.

Agamemnon to Clytaemnestra

Sunium

Dear Clytaemnestra,

We have had a very good journey, and I shall reach Mycenae the day after tomorrow in the morning. Please have a hot bath ready for me. I am bringing Cassandra with me. She had better have the room looking north, as she hates the sun. She is very nervous and upset, and you must be kind to her.

Your loving husband,
Agamemnon.

Odysseus to Penelope

The Island of Ogygia

Dearest Penelope,

We arrived here after a very tiresome voyage. I will not tire you with the details, which are numerous and technical. The net result is that the local physician says I cannot proceed with my

95

journey until I am thoroughly rested. This spot is pleasant, but the only society I have is that of poor dear Calypso. She means well and is most hospitable, but you can imagine how vexed I am by this delay and the intolerable tedium of this enforced repose. Kiss Telemachus from me.

Your loving husband,
Odysseus.

Clytaemnestra to Aegisthus

I am sending this by runner. Come back directly. I expect Agamemnon any moment. The bonfires are already visible. Please bring a good strong net and a sharp axe with you. I will explain when you arrive. I have quite decided that half measures are out of the question.

C.

A
Christmas
Cracker

1983

Sir,

Mrs Thatcher is quite right to condemn the unhygienic custom of baby-handling by electioneering parliamentary candidates.

My son was sitting in his perambulator, harmlessly surveying the sea at Criccieth, when he was patted on the head by Mr Lloyd George. He was bald before he was 30.

R. Neville
Crowborough, Sussex

Sir William Davenant became Poet Laureate of England after the death of Ben Jonson. I know two interesting things about him. First, he liked to think that he was the illegitimate son of Shakespeare – which he may well have been, since his father kept the Crown Inn at Oxford, where Shakespeare always put up on his journeys between Stratford and London. Second, he had no nose; as John Aubrey explains, 'He gott a terrible clap of a Black handsome wench that lay in Axe-yard, Westminster . . . which cost him his Nose, with which unlucky mischance many witts were too cruelly bold.'

He was not in the first league, as poets go; but he wrote this lovely song:

> The lark now leaves his wat'ry nest,
>   And climbing, shakes his dewy wings;
> He takes this window for the east,
>   And to implore your light, he sings,
> Awake, awake, the morn will never rise
> Till she can dress her beauty at your eyes.
>
> The merchant bows unto the seaman's star,
>   The ploughman from the sun his season takes;
> But still the lover wonders what they are,
>   Who look for day before his mistress wakes.
> Awake, awake, break through your veils of lawn,
> Then draw your curtains, and begin the dawn.

One of the contemporary English novelists most admired by Henry James was George Eliot. He called on her one Sunday afternoon in 1869 and found her

. . . magnificently ugly – deliciously hideous. She has a low fore-head, a dull grey eye, a vast pendulous nose, a huge mouth, full of uneven teeth and a chin and jaw-bone *qui n'en finissent pas* . . . Now in this vast ugliness resides a most powerful beauty which, in a very few minutes, steals forth and charms the mind, so that you end as I ended, in falling in love with her. Yes, behold me literally in love with this great horse-faced bluestocking.

In my father's diary of 12 March 1919 he notes:

Augustine Birrell told how Henry James was once asked what were the sensations of Cross [the man twenty-two years her junior whom she married after the death of her long-time lover G. H. Lewes] when George Eliot died. He answered, after deep thought and with a great effort to find the exact word: 'Grief – grief – regret – remorse – *relief.*'

Another of James's favourites – though for rather different reasons – was Rupert Brooke, to whose posthumously-published Letters from America *he wrote the preface. The best comment on this is to be found in the diary of A. C. Benson:*

What nonsense it is, to be sure. H. J. hadn't much to say except that R. B. was a cheerful and high-spirited boy who lived in many ways a normal life, enjoyed himself, was not spoilt, and then wrote some fine bits of poetry. All this is presented in long, vague, sentences, very confusing and Johnsonian, with an occa-sional scrap of slang let in. It *isn't* good writing – of that I am sure. Then come a lot of jolly, ordinary, sensible, wholesome, rather funny letters of travel by R. B. After all H. J.'s pontifica-tion, dim with incense-smoke, stately, mysterious, R. B.'s robust letters are almost a shock. It is as if one went up to receive a sacrament in a great, dark church, and were greeted by shouts of laughter and a shower of chocolate creams.

Queen Elizabeth I, to the Judges of the Realm:

Have a care over my people. You have my people – do that which I ought to do. They are *my* people. Every man oppresseth them and spoileth them without mercy; they cannot revenge their quarrel, nor help themselves. See unto them, see unto them, for they are my charge. I charge you, even as God has charged me.

In Evelyn Waugh's early travel book, Labels, *he tells of a visit to Paris, during which his attention was suddenly caught by*

the spectacle of a man in the Place Beauveau, who had met with an accident which must, I think, be unique. He was a man of middle age and, to judge by his bowler hat and frock coat, of the official class, and his umbrella had caught alight. I do not know how this can have happened. I passed him in a taxi-cab, and saw him in the centre of a small crowd, grasping it still by the handle and holding it at arm's length so that the flames should not scorch him. It was a dry day and the umbrella burnt flamboyantly. I followed the scene as long as I could from the little window in the back of the car, and saw him finally drop the handle and push it, with his foot, into the gutter. It lay there smoking, and the crowd peered at it curiously before moving off. A London crowd would have thought that the best possible joke, but none of the witnesses laughed, and no one to whom I have told this story in England has believed a word of it.

Kingsley Amis subsequently wrote to me:

On the mystery of the blazing umbrella I can throw a little light. I once tossed a burning cigarette-butt into the air, swiped negligently at it with my furled but not rolled umbrella and, having presumably managed to trap it instead of deflecting it, was soon much troubled by smoke and fumes. (Doubly discomfiting since by now I had reached the SCR in St John's.)

Dante, in the Sixth Canto of the Inferno, *thus describes the third circle of Hell:*

Io sono al terzo cerchio de la piova
　　Eterna, maladetta, fredda e greve
　　Regola e qualità mai non l'è nova.
Grandine grossa, acqua tinta e neve
　　Per l'aere tenebroso si riversa;
　　Pute la terra che questo riceve.

– lines which might be translated:

I stand in that third circle, where the rain
Falls merciless, malignant, bitter cold,
Unvaried in its fury and its force.
Black waters, driving hail and swirling snow
Commingle in the dark, distempered air,
Making the sad earth reek, whereon they fall.

Is there, I wonder, any record of Dante's having visited London in the spring?

I found a White Russian general living nearby, a handsome, fine-mannered man whose white hair flowed down to a military beard. Aide-de-camp once to Czar Nicholas II, he had brought the remnant of the Imperial Cossack Guard into Yugoslavia when the war was lost, and there they had worked on the railways for a while before disbanding for ever. A liturgical reader now, he chanted in the church with the nuns, and looked after his delicate wife with masculine gentleness.

'The past is finished,' he said, smiling. 'Why dwell on these things? They are fifty years away, and all our lives have happened in between. In heaven I will not say "I was a general to the Czar of all the Russias"; I will tell them that I was a reader here in the church of St Mary Magdalene.'

He bent near to catch my answer, for he was almost deaf, and I shouted approval.

'To tell the truth,' he said, 'I am not much proud of my youth. But luckily one forgets. Now we are just two old people ending our lives. We are content and we look to God.' He smiled at his wife, as if their happiness were a secret. 'So you are a writer? Have you heard our Christmas services? They, at least, are worth writing of. But don't speak of our past: nobody is interested in that any more. Only say, if you like, that you heard an old man singing in the Russian church at Gethsemane.'

If he should read this, I hope he will forgive me.

Colin Thubron
Jerusalem

From Denis Healey comes this extract from the Modern Polyglot Conversational Italian *(with Dictionary) published by G. Alfano of Naples. The
date is uncertain, but almost certainly somewhere in the inter-war years. I
omit the parallel Italian translation.*

– Be quick and put on my wrapper and a white napkin, and
strap [*sic*] your razors when you have lathered me.

– Ah! you have put the brush into my mouth.

– It was because you spoke when I did not expect it. The
young bride's hair was black, thick, coarse, her forehead broad
and square. An ordinary hairdresser would not have been able to
hide the sternness of her features; but I have given her head a
gentle and languishing expression.

– Truly, I am struck with admiration. But, mister artist, with
all your talent you have cut me; I am bleeding. You have been
shaving against the grain.

– No, sir; I have only taken off a little pimple. With a bit of
courtplaster, it will not be seen.

– Doesn't my hair need to be freshened up a little?

– I will cut a little off behind; but I would not touch the tuft
on the forehead nor about the ears.

– Why not?

– Because, sir, you would then appear to have too low a
forehead and ears too long. Do you wish me to give you a touch
of the curling irons, sir?

– It is unnecessary; my hair curls naturally.

– Shall I put on a little oil or pomatum?

– Put on a little scented oil.

– Please look in the glass.

– It will do very well. I see you are an artist worthy to shave
and trim your contemporaries.

We all know Rosalind's words in As You Like It:

Time travels in divers paces, with divers persons. I'll tell you who Time ambles withal, who Time trots withal, who Time gallops withal, and who he stands still withal.

I was reminded of them when my friend John Guest sent me this verse, inscribed on the pendulum of the clock in St Lawrence's church, Bidborough, Kent:

When as a child I laughed and wept,
  Time crept
When as a youth I dreamed and talked,
  Time walked
When I became a full-grown man,
  Time ran
And later as I older grew,
  Time flew.
Soon shall I find when travelling on
  Time gone.
Will Christ have saved my soul by then?
  Amen.

In 1974 I included in the Cracker a quotation from a book called Health's Improvement: Or, Rules Comprizing and Discovering the Nature, Method and Manner of Preparing all sorts of FOOD used in this Nation, *by 'that ever Famous Thomas Muffett, Doctor in Physick'. (Dr Muffett was also, in his day, the leading authority on insects – an expertise not, alas, shared by his daughter Patience who became the world's most celebrated arachnophobe.) The following further extracts are taken from the 1655 edition, 'corrected and enlarged' by Dr Christopher Bennet, Fellow of the 'College of Physitians' in London.*

Swans flesh was forbidden the Jewes, because by them the Hieroglyphical Sages did describe hypocrisie; for as Swans have the whitest feathers and the blackest flesh of all birds, so the heart of *Hypocrites* is contrary to their outward appearance.

So that not for the badness of their flesh, but for resembling of wicked men's minds they were forbidden: for being young they are not the worst of meats; nay if they be kept in a little pound and well fed with Corn, their flesh will not only alter the blackness, but also be freed of the unwholesomeness; Being thus used, they are appointed to be the first dish at the Emperour of *Muscovie* his table, and also much esteemed in East-Friezland.

Cuttles (called also sleeves for their shape, and scribes for their incky humour wherewith they are replenished) are commended by *Galen* for great nourishers; their skins be as smooth as any womans, but their flesh as brawny as any ploughmans, therefore I fear me *Galen* rather commended them upon hearsay, than upon any just cause or true experience; *Apicius*, that great Mastercook, makes sausages of them with lard and other things; which composition I would not have omitted, if it had been worth the penning.

Puffins, whom I may call the feathered fishes, are accounted even by the holy fatherhood of Cardinals to be no flesh but rather fish; whose Catholique censure I will not here oppugne, though I have just reason for it, because I will not encrease the Popes Coffers; which no doubt would be filled, if every Puffin eater bought a pardon, upon true and certain knowledge that a Puffin were flesh: albeit perhaps if his Holiness would say, that a shoulder of Muton were fish, they either would not or could not think it flesh.

> . . . Now does he feel
> His secret murders sticking on his hands.

A line and a half from Macbeth *that I can never hear without a frisson. What a glorious play it is to read, and yet how rarely it seems to succeed on the stage – I suspect because so few actors or producers follow the advice of John Masefield:*

> Let your Macbeth be chosen for the nervy, fiery beauty of his power. He must have tense intelligence, a swift, leaping, lovely body, and a voice able to exalt and to blast. Let him not play the earlier scenes like a moody traitor, but like Lucifer, star of the morning. Let him not play the later scenes like a hangman who has taken to drink, but like an angel who has fallen.

[This compares interestingly with Verdi's views about Lady Macbeth. Before his opera was first put on in Naples in 1848, with the great Eugenia Tadolini singing Lady Macbeth, he explained his misgivings:

> Mme Tadolini looks beautiful and good, and I should like Lady Macbeth to look ugly and evil. Mme Tadolini sings to perfection, and I should like Lady Macbeth not to sing at all. Mme Tadolini has a stupendous voice, clear, limpid, powerful: I should like in Lady Macbeth a voice rough, hoarse and gloomy. Mme Tadolini's voice has angelic qualities; I should like the voice of Lady Macbeth to have something diabolical about it.*]*

On the wall in Symphony Hall, Boston, Mass., there is a plaque which reads

In Memory of
the Devoted Musicians
Wallace Henry Hartley, Bandmaster
John Frederick Preston Clark
Percy Cornelius Taylor
John Wesley Woodward
W. Theodore Brailey
John Law Hume
Georges Krins
Roger Bricoux

Who were drowned
Still playing
As the Titanic went down
April 15, 1912.

A similar plaque can be seen in the Philharmonic Hall, Liverpool. Below the names – two of which are spelt slightly differently – the inscription here runs

Members of the band on board the 'Titanic'. They bravely continued playing to soothe the anguish of their fellow passengers until the ship sank in the deep.

April 14th [*sic*] 1912.

Courage and Compassion joined make the hero and the man complete.

How much better is the American version: simple and short, without a wasted word.

[This plaque was, I have since learnt, put up by the famous Mrs Isabella Stewart Gardner of Boston, who can presumably also be credited with the wording. 'Sadly,' writes my friend Bump Hadley, former director of the Gardner Museum, 'I know nothing more about it, or why she did it, except that she was often found doing things that others wished they had done.'

My dear friend the late Jack Lambert of the Sunday Times, *who always acknowledged the Cracker with a poem, subsequently sent me the following:*

Wallace Henry Hartley
Flicked his baton smartly.
Next, there sounds so bravely – hark!
John Frederick Preston Clark
And that most melodious sailor
Percy Cornelius Taylor.
Never – he was much too good – warred
With harmony John Wesley Woodward.
Over the waves there fluttered gaily
To cheer us the strains of Theodore Brailey.
Ignoring the threat of impending doom
Gallantly on played John Law Hume.
Always expansive, never *mince*,
Out sang the comfort of Georges Krins;
And last of this octet's noble number
Roger Bricoux still plays as they slumber.

Are they all playing still in their deep-sea beds,
The ocean surging over their heads,
Their ghostly prayer but faintly heard
By none but a cod or a passing bird? /

In the late autumn of 1955 my cousin Rupert Hart-Davis, writing to his friend George Lyttelton, reminded him of the poem Thomas Hardy had written on the Titanic disaster, 'The Convergence of the Twain'. On 7 December, George replied:

. . . Gosh, yes, that *Titanic* poem! I remember the thing happening. I was dining with the Head Master [of Eton] and Mrs Warre came in quivering slightly with age and dottiness, and said 'I am sorry to hear there has been a bad boating accident' – an odd but very characteristic way of describing the sinking of the largest ship in the world and the death of 1,400 people. How trivial Hardy continually makes the moderns look and sound. *Of course* 'An Ancient to Ancients' hits my feeling in every line, and in fact might have been written by me, if I had had the mind – as C. Lamb delightedly reported Wordsworth as saying about himself and the plays of Shakespeare. You remember of course Hardy's 'Reminiscences of a Dancing Man' in *Time's Laughing-Stocks* and its magnificently innocent first line. ['Who now remembers Almack's balls.'] Once in a *New Statesman* competition, something about lines or phrases which meant *now* something quite different from what they meant originally, I sent up the last three lines of his 'The Caged Goldfinch' in *Moments of Vision*. It was mentioned, but I won no prize.

The three lines in question read:

And some at times averred
The grave to be her false one's, who when wooing
Gave her the bird.

The *Narcissus*, heeling over to off-shore gusts, rounded the South Foreland, passed through the Downs and, in tow, entered the river. Shorn of the glory of her white wings, she wound obediently after the tug through the maze of invisible channels. As she passed them the red-painted light-vessels, swung at their moorings, seemed for an instant to sail with great speed in the rush of tide, and the next moment were left hopelessly behind. The big buoys on the tails of banks slipped past her sides very low, and, dropping in her wake, tugged at their chains like fierce watch-dogs. The reach narrowed; from both sides the land approached the ship. She went steadily up the river. On the riverside slopes the houses appeared in groups – seemed to stream down the declivities at a run to see her pass, and, checked by the mud of the foreshore, crowded on the banks. Further on, the tall factory chimneys appeared in insolent bands and watched her go by, like a struggling crowd of slim giants, swaggering and upright under the black plummets of smoke, cavalierly aslant. She swept round the bends; an impure breeze shrieked a welcome between her stripped spars; and the land, closing in, stepped between the ship and the sea.

A low cloud hung before her – a great opalescent and tremulous cloud, that seemed to rise from the steaming brows of millions of men. Long drifts of smoky vapours soiled it with livid trails; it throbbed to the beat of millions of hearts, and from it came an immense and lamentable murmur – the murmur of millions of lips praying, cursing, sighing, jeering – the undying murmur of folly, regret, and hope exhaled by the crowds of the anxious earth. The *Narcissus* entered the cloud; the shadows deepened; on all sides there was the clang of iron, the sound of mighty blows, shrieks, yells. Black barges drifted stealthily on the murky stream. A mad jumble of begrimed walls loomed up vaguely in the smoke, bewildering and mournful, like a vision of disaster. The tugs, panting furiously, backed and filled in the stream, to hold the ship steady at the dock-gates; from her bows two lines went through the air whistling, and struck at the land viciously, like a pair of snakes. A bridge broke in two before her, as if by enchantment; big hydraulic capstans began to turn all by themselves, as though animated by a mysterious and unholy spell. She moved through a narrow lane of water between two low walls of granite, and men with check-ropes in their hands kept pace with her, walking on the broad flagstones. . . .

'Let go your quarter-checks! Let go!' sang out a ruddy-faced old man on the quay. The ropes heavily falling in the water, and the *Narcissus* entered the dock.

Joseph Conrad
The Nigger of the Narcissus

Whose love is given over well
Shall look on Helen's face in Hell;
But he whose love is thin and wise
Shall see John Knox in Paradise.

Dorothy Parker

Toutes choses sont dites déjà, mais comme personne n'écoute, il faut toujours recommencer.

André Gide

Few novels have a better opening sentence than **Persuasion***:*

Sir Walter Elliot, of Kellynch-Hall, in Somersetshire, was a man
who, for his own amusement, never took up any book but the
Baronetage; there he found occupation for an idle hour, and
consolation in a distressed one; there his faculties were roused
into admiration and respect, by contemplating the limited remnant
of the earliest patents; there any unwelcome sensations, arising
from domestic affairs, changed naturally into pity and contempt,
as he turned over the almost endless creations of the last century
– and there, if every other leaf were powerless, he could read his
own history with an interest which never failed – this was the
page at which the favourite volume always opened:

> 'ELLIOT OF KELLYNCH-HALL.'

Tennyson took a rather different view:

No little lily-handed Baronet he,
A great broad-shouldered genial Englishman.

> *The Princess*

*In the 1977 Cracker I quoted Lord Grey of Falloden on Jane Austen. His
opinion was rather neatly paraphrased by Somerset Maugham when he
wrote (in* Ten Novels and Their Authors*):*

Nothing very much happens in her books, and yet, when you
come to the bottom of a page, you eagerly turn it to learn what
will happen next. Nothing very much does and again you eagerly
turn the page. The novelist who has the power to achieve this has
the most precious gift a novelist can possess.

*Very true. But there are other gifts with which Miss Austen was, arguably,
less well endowed. I do not think that it was professional jealousy that
caused Charlotte Brontë to write, in a letter of 1850 to W. S. Williams:*

Her business is not half so much with the human heart as with
the human eyes, mouth, hands and feet; what sees keenly, speaks
aptly, moves flexibly, it suits her to study; but what throbs fast
and full, though hidden, what the blood rushes through, what is
the unseen seat of Life and the sentient target of Death – *this*
Miss Austen ignores ... Jane Austen was a complete and most
sensible lady, but a very incomplete and rather insensible (*not
senseless*) woman. If this is heresy, I cannot help it.

Today we have naming of parts. Yesterday
We had daily cleaning. And tomorrow morning
We shall have what to do after firing. But today,
Today we have naming of parts. Japonica
Glistens like coral in all of the neighbouring gardens,
    And today we have naming of parts.

This is the lower sling swivel. And this
Is the upper sling swivel, whose use you will see,
When you are given your slings. And this is the piling swivel,
Which in your case you have not got. The branches
Hold in the gardens their silent, eloquent gestures,
    Which in our case we have not got.

This is the safety-catch, which is always released
With an easy flick of the thumb. And please do not let me
See anyone using his finger. You can do it quite easy
If you have any strength in your thumb. The blossoms
Are fragile and motionless, never letting anyone see
    Any of them using their finger.

And this you can see is the bolt. The purpose of this
Is to open the breech, as you see. We can slide it
Rapidly backwards and forwards: we call this
Easing the spring. And rapidly backwards and forwards
The early bees are assaulting and fumbling the flowers:
    They call it easing the Spring.

They call it easing the Spring: it is perfectly easy
If you have any strength in your thumb: like the bolt,
And the breech, and the cocking-piece, and the point of
    balance,
Which in our case we have not got; and the almond-blossom
Silent in all of the gardens and the bees going backwards and
    forwards,
    For today we have naming of parts.

                    Henry Reed

April and May are the best walking months in Italy. Carry water in a flask, for it is sometimes ten miles from one well to the next that you may chance to find. A siesta in the shade for three or four hours in the mid-day heat, to the tune of cicada and nightingale, is not the least pleasant part of all; and that means early starting and night walking at the end, both very good things. The stars out there rule the sky more than in England, big and lustrous with the honour of having shone upon the ancients and been named by them. On Italian mountain-tops we stand on naked, pagan earth, under the heaven of Lucretius:

> *Luna, dies, et nox, et noctis signa severa.*

The chorus-ending from Aristophanes' *Frogs*, raised every night from every ditch that drains into the Mediterranean, hoarse and primeval as a raven's croak, is one of the grandest tunes to walk by. Or on a night in May one can walk through the too rare Italian forests for an hour on end and never be out of hearing of the nightingales' song.

G. M. Trevelyan
'Walking', in *Clio, a Muse*

*The French versifier – he would never, I think, have called himself a poet –
Alphonse Allais waged a life-long battle with the French language. Or was
it a love affair? Or, perhaps, both? What he liked best was puns, the more
outlandish the better, which is why I love him.*

> Sans la moindre mitaine,
> Il lit l'oeuvre de Taine.
>
> Son thon de l'aquarium
> S'évade et file à Riom.
>
> A son excellent père
> Il parle avec colère.
>
> Surveille mieux, fiston,
> Ton thon, ton Taine et ton ton.

Here is another:

> Il répétait souvent: 'La reine est un chameau
> Funeste.' On l'envoya ramer sur la galère
> Du roi. Jusqu'à sa mort, il ne dit plus un mot.
>   L'embarquement pour s'y taire.

And the Lord said unto Noah, where is the ark, which I commanded thee to build? And Noah said unto the Lord, Verily, I have had three carpenters off sick. The gopher-wood supplier hath let me down – yea, even though the gopher wood hath been on order for nigh upon twelve months. The damp-course specialist hath not turned up. What can I do, O Lord?

And God said unto Noah, I want that ark finished even after seven days and seven nights. And Noah said, It will be so. And it was not so.

And the Lord said unto Noah, What seemeth to be the trouble this time? And Noah said unto the Lord, Mine subcontractor hath gone bankrupt. The pitch which thou commandest me to put on the outside and on the inside of the ark hath not arrived ... The glazier departeth on holiday in Majorca – yea, even though I offerest him double time. Shem, my son, who helpeth me on the ark side of the business, hath formed a pop group with his brothers Ham and Japeth. Lord, I am undone.

And God said in his wrath, Noah, do not thou mucketh Me about ... And Noah said, Lo, the contract will be fulfilled. And Lo, it was not fulfilled.

And Noah said unto the Lord, The gopher wood is definitely in the warehouse. Verily, and the gopher-wood supplier waiteth only upon his servant to find the invoices before he delivereth the gopher wood unto me. And the Lord grew angry and said, Scrubbeth thou round the gopher wood. What about the animals? ... And Noah said, the van cometh on Tuesday; yea and yea, it will be so. And the Lord said unto Noah, how about the unicorns?

And Noah wrung his hands and wept, saying, Lord, Lord, they are a discontinued line. Thou canst not get unicorns for love nor money.

And God said unto Noah, Thou hast not made an ark of gopher wood, nor hast thou lined it with pitch within and without; and of every living thing of all flesh, two of every sort hast thou failed to bring into the ark. What sayest thou, Noah? And Noah kissed the earth and said, Lord, Lord, thou knowest in thy wisdom what it is like with delivery dates.

And the Lord in his wisdom said, Noah, my son, I knowest. Why else dost thou think I have caused a flood?

[This wry little piece was read, with a few variants, by Celia Johnson in an anthology programme which she compiled for the BBC; she did not know the author, and nor did I when I included it in the Cracker. I have, however, since discovered that it is by Keith Waterhouse – to whom I apologize for so belated an acknowledgement. The text as given above is the authentic one, slightly abridged for reasons of space.]

The piers are pummelled by the waves;
In a lonely field the rain
Lashes an abandoned train;
Outlaws fill the mountain caves.

Fantastic grow the evening gowns;
Agents of the Fisc pursue
Absconding tax-defaulters through
The sewers of provincial towns.

Private rites of magic send
The temple prostitutes to sleep;
All the literati keep
An imaginary friend.

Cerebotonic Catos may
Extol the Ancient Disciplines,
But the muscle-bound Marines
Mutiny for food and pay.

Caesar's double bed is warm
As an unimportant clerk
Writes I DO NOT LIKE MY WORK
On a pink official form.

Unendowed with wealth or pity,
Little birds with scarlet legs,
Sitting on their speckled eggs,
Eye each flu-infected city.

Altogether elsewhere, vast
Herds of reindeer move across
Miles and miles of golden moss,
Silently and very fast.

W. H. Auden

Abandoned railways seem to have had a particular message for Auden. In 'The Letter' occur the equally haunting lines:

> . . . Shall see, shall pass, as we have seen
> The swallow on the tile, spring's green
> Preliminary shiver, passed
> A solitary truck, the last
> Of shunting in the Autumn.

In 'The Quest,' too, there is a line

> This empty junction glitters in the sun

which sticks strangely firm in my memory.

Dr William Harvey published his great work De Motu Cordis – *in which he announced his discovery of the circulation of the blood – in 1628. Twenty-three years later, in 1651, he produced another work,* De Generatione Animalium. *He wrote it in Latin; the following passage is taken from the anonymous English translation which was published soon afterwards. It describes the mating habits of the cock and the hen.*

The Males when they arm themselves, and are in all respects well appointed for Loves encounter, how strangely doth the potent Cupid heighten their inflamed spirits, how spruce are they, how do they pride in it; how vigorous, how testy are they, and prone to conflicts! But when this office and performance ceaseth: Oh! how soon doth their force abate, and their late fury coole! how do they hale in all their swelling sails, and check their daring! Nay even while this jocund Sacrifice to Venus is in season, no sooner is the act performed, but they grow tame and pusillanimous; as if it were then deep printed in their thoughts, that while they impart a life to others, they are in full career to their own urnes. Onely our Cock, full fraught with seed and spirits, approves himself the onely cheerfull loser, and with the plaudit of his wings and voice, crownes his past triumphs, and lights his wedding Torch at his own Cinders. And yet he also flags after long game, and like an Emerit souldier resigns his Commission. And so the Hens likewise, like Plants worn out, grow decayed Matrons, and fore-go their Nurseries.

SONG IN THE OLD MANNER

C'est ma Jeunesse qui s'en va.
Adieu! la très gente compagne –
Oncques ne suis moins gai pour ça
(C'est ma Jeunesse qui s'en va)
Et lon-lon-laire, et lon-lon là,
Peut-être perds; peut-être gagne.
C'est ma Jeunesse qui s'en va.

Hilaire Belloc

BONUS

Depending on what you feel about Kipling, you will think 'The Mary Gloster' – perhaps more of a novel than a poem – one of his best or one of his worst. I was brought up on it and love it: so did my father, one of whose greatest treats it was to be asked to read it aloud after dinner, though he nearly always seized up half-way through, and finished (if at all) with the tears pouring down his cheeks.

THE MARY GLOSTER

I've paid for your sickest fancies; I've humoured your crackedest
    whim –
Dick, it's your daddy, dying; you've got to listen to him!
Good for a fortnight, am I? The doctor told you? He lied.
I shall go under by morning, and – Put that nurse outside.
'Never seen death yet, Dickie? Well, now is your time to learn,
And you'll wish you held my record before it comes to your turn.
Not counting the Line and the Foundry, the yards and the
    village, too,
I've made myself a million; but I'm damned if I made you.
Master at two-and-twenty, and married at twenty-three –
Ten thousand men on the pay-roll, and forty freighters at sea!
Fifty years between 'em, and every year of it fight,
And now I'm Sir Anthony Gloster, dying, a baronite:
For I lunched with his Royal 'Ighness – what was it the papers
    a-had?
'Not least of our merchant-princes.' Dickie, that's me, your dad!
I didn't begin with askings. *I* took my job and I stuck;
And I took the chances they wouldn't, an' now they're calling it
    luck.
Lord, what boats I've handled – rotten and leaky and old!
Ran 'em, or – opened the bilge-cock, precisely as I was told.
Grub that 'ud bind you crazy, and crews that 'ud turn you grey,
And a big fat lump of insurance to cover the risk on the way.
The others they dursn't do it; they said they valued their life
(They've served me since as skippers). *I* went, and I took my wife.
Over the world I drove 'em, married at twenty-three,
And your mother saving the money and making a man of me,
I was content to be master, but she said there was better
    behind;
She took the chances I wouldn't, and I followed your mother
    blind.
She egged me to borrow the money, an' she helped me to clear
    the loan,
When we bought half shares in a cheap 'un and hoisted a flag
    of our own.

Patching and coaling on credit, and living the Lord knew how,
We started the Red Ox freighters – we've eight-and-thirty now.
And those were the days of clippers, and the freights were
      clipper-freights,
And we knew we were making our fortune, but she died in
      Macassar Straits –
By the Little Paternosters, as you come to the Union Bank –
And we dropped her in fourteen fathom; I pricked it off where
      she sank.
Owners we were, full owners, and the boat was christened for her,
And she died in the Mary Gloster. My heart, how young we were!
So I went on a spree round Java and well-nigh ran her ashore,
But your mother came and warned me and I wouldn't liquor
      no more:
Strict I stuck to my business, afraid to stop or I'd think,
Saving the money (she warned me), and letting the other men
      drink.
And I met M'Cullough in London (I'd turned five 'undred then),
And 'tween us we started the Foundry – three forges and twenty
      men:
Cheap repairs for the cheap 'uns. It paid, and the business grew,
For I bought me a steam-lathe patent, and that was a gold
      mine too.
'Cheaper to build 'em then buy 'em,' *I* said, but M'Cullough
      he shied,
And we wasted a year in talking before we moved to the Clyde.
And the Lines were all beginning, and we all of us started fair,
Building our engines like houses and staying the boilers square.
But M'Cullough 'e wanted cabins with marble and maple and all,
And Brussels an' Utrecht velvet, and baths and a Social Hall,
And pipes for closets all over, and cutting the frames too light,
But M'Cullough he died in the Sixties, and – Well, I'm dying
      tonight . . .
I knew – *I* knew what was coming, when we bid on the *Byfleet's*
      keel –
They piddled and piffled with iron: I'd given my orders for
      steel!
Steel and the first expansions. It paid, I tell you, it paid,
When we came with our nine-knot freighters and collared the
      long-run trade!
And they asked me how I did it, and I gave 'em the Scripture
      text,
'You keep your light so shining a little in front o' the next!'
They copied all they could follow, but they couldn't copy my
      mind,
And I left 'em sweating and stealing a year and a half behind.

Then came the armour-contracts, but that was M'Cullough's
   side;
He was always best in the Foundry, but better, perhaps, he died.
I went through his private papers; the notes was plainer than
   print;
And I'm no fool to finish if a man'll give me a hint.
(I remember his widow was angry.) So I saw what the drawings
   meant,
And I started the six-inch rollers, and it paid me sixty per cent –
Sixty per cent *with* failures, and more than twice we could do,
And a quarter-million to credit, and I saved it all for you!
I thought – it doesn't matter – you seemed to favour your ma,
But you're nearer forty than thirty, and I know the kind you are.
Harrer an' Trinity College! I ought to ha' sent you to sea –
But I stood you an education, an' what have you done for me?
The things I knew was proper you wouldn't thank me to give,
And the things I knew was rotten you said was the way to live.
For you muddled with books and pictures, an' china an' etchin's
   an' fans,
And your rooms at college was beastly – more like a whore's
   than a man's –
Till you married that thin-flanked woman, as white and as stale
   as a bone,
An' she gave you your social nonsense; but where's that kid o'
   your own?
I've seen your carriages blocking the half o' the Cromwell Road,
But never the doctor's brougham to help the missus unload.
(So there isn't even a grandchild, an' the Gloster family's done.)
Not like your mother, she isn't. *She* carried her freight each run.
But they died, the pore little beggars! At sea she had 'em –
   they died.
Only you, an' you stood it; you haven't stood much beside.
Weak, a liar, and idle, and mean as a collier's whelp
Nosing for scraps in the galley. No help – my son was no help!
So he gets three 'undred thousand, in trust and the interest paid.
I wouldn't give it you, Dickie – you see, I made it in trade.
You're saved from soiling your fingers, and if you have no child,
It all comes back to the business. Gad, won't your wife be wild!
'Calls and calls in her carriage, her 'andkerchief up to 'er eye:
'Daddy! dear daddy's dyin'!' and doing her best to cry.
Grateful? Oh, yes, I'm grateful, but keep her away from here.
Your mother 'ud never ha' stood 'er, and, anyhow, women are
   queer . . .
There's women will say I've married a second time. Not quite!
But give pore Aggie a hundred, and tell her your lawyers'll
   fight.

She was the best o' the boiling – you'll meet her before it ends;
I'm in for a row with the mother – I'll leave you settle my
      friends:
For a man he must go with a woman, which women don't
      understand –
Or the sort that say they can see it they aren't the marrying brand.
But I wanted to speak o' your mother that's Lady Gloster still –
I'm going to up and see her, without it's hurting the will.
Here! Take your hand off the bell-pull. Five thousand's waiting
      for you,
If you'll only listen a minute, and do as I bid you do.
They'll try to prove me crazy, and, if you bungle, they can;
And I've only you to trust to! (O God, why ain't he a man?)
There's some waste money on marbles, the same as M'Cullough
      tried –
Marbles and mausoleums – but I call that sinful pride.
There's some ship bodies for burial – we've carried 'em, soldered
      and packed;
Down in their wills they wrote it, and nobody called *them*
      cracked.
But me – I've too much money, and people might . . . All my
      fault:
It came o' hoping for grandsons and buying that Wokin' vault.
I'm sick o' the 'ole dam' business; I'm going back where I came.
Dick, you're the son o' my body, and you'll take charge o' the same!
I want to lie by your mother, ten thousand mile away,
And they'll want to send me to Woking; and that's where you'll
      earn your pay.
I've thought it out on the quiet, the same as it ought to be done –
Quiet, and decent, and proper – an' here's your orders, my son.
You know the Line? You don't, though. You write to the Board,
      and tell
Your father's death has upset you an' you're goin' to cruise for
      a spell,
An' you'd like the Mary Gloster – I've held her ready for this –
They'll put her in working order and you'll take her out as she is.
Yes, it was money idle when I patched her and put her aside
(Thank God, I can pay for my fancies!) – the boat where your
      mother died,
By the Little Paternosters, as you come to the Union Bank,
We dropped her – I think I told you – and I pricked it off where
      she sank –
['Tiny she looked on the grating – that oily, treacly sea –]
'Hundred and eighteen East, remember, and South just three.
Easy bearings to carry – three South – three to the dot;
But I gave M'Andrew a copy in case of dying – or not.

And so you'll write to M'Andrew, he's Chief of the Maori Line;
They'll give him leave, if you ask 'em and say it's business o'
    mine.
I built three boats for the Maoris, an' very well pleased they were,
An' I've known Mac since the Fifties, and Mac knew me – and
    her.
After the first stroke warned me I sent him the money to keep
Against the time you'd claim it, committin' your dad to the deep;
For you are the son o' my body, and Mac was my oldest friend,
I've never asked 'im to dinner, but he'll see it out to the end.
Stiff-necked Glasgow beggar, I've heard he's prayed for my soul,
But he couldn't lie if you paid him, and he'd starve before he
    stole!
He'll take the Mary in ballast – you'll find her a lively ship;
And you'll take Sir Anthony Gloster, that goes on 'is wedding-
    trip.
Lashed in our old deck-cabin with all three port-holes wide,
The kick o' the screw beneath him and the round blue seas
    outside!
Sir Anthony Gloster's carriage – our 'ouse-flag flyin' free –
Ten thousand men on the pay-roll and forty freighters at sea!
He made himself and a million, but this world is a fleetin' show,
And he'll go the wife of 'is bosom the same as he ought to go –
By the heel of the Paternosters – there isn't a chance to mistake –
And Mac'll pay you the money as soon as the bubbles break!
Five thousand for six weeks' cruising, the stanchest freighter
    afloat,
And Mac he'll give you your bonus the minute I'm out o' the
    boat!
He'll take you round to Macassar, and you'll come back alone;
He knows what I want o' the Mary . . . I'll do what I please with
    my own.
Your mother 'ud call it wasteful, but I've seven-and-thirty more;
I'll come in my private carriage and bid it wait at the door . . .
For my son 'e was never a credit: 'e muddled with books and art,
And 'e lived on Sir Anthony's money and 'e broke Sir Anthony's
    heart.
There isn't even a grandchild, and the Gloster family's done –
The only one you left me, O mother, the only one!
Harrer and Trinity College – me slavin' early an' late –
An' he thinks I'm dying crazy, and you're in Macassar Strait!
Flesh o' my flesh, my dearie, for ever an' ever amen,
That first stroke come for a warning; I ought to ha' gone to you
    then.
But – cheap repairs for a cheap 'un – the doctors said I'd do:
Mary, why didn't *you* warn me? I've allus heeded to you,

Excep' – I know – about women; but you are a spirit now;
An', wife, they was only women, and I was a man. That's how.
An' a man 'e must go with a woman, as you could not understand;
But I never talked 'em secrets. I paid 'em out o' hand.
Thank Gawd, I can pay for my fancies! Now what's five
      thousand to me,
For a berth off the Paternosters in the haven where I would be?
I believe in the Resurrection, if I read my Bible plain,
But I wouldn't trust 'em at Wokin'; we're safer at sea again.
For the heart it shall go with the treasure – go down to the sea
      in ships.
I'm sick of the hired women – I'll kiss my girl on her lips!
I'll be content with my fountain, I'll drink from my own well,
And the wife of my youth shall charm me – an' the rest can go
      to Hell!
(Dickie, *he* will, that's certain.) I'll lie in our standin'-bed,
An' Mac'll take her in ballast – an' she trims best by the head . . .
Down by the head an' sinkin', her fires are drawn and cold,
And the water's splashin' hollow on the skin of the empty
      hold –
Churning an' choking and chuckling, quiet and scummy and
      dark –
Full to her lower hatches and risin' steady. Hark!
That was the after-bulkhead . . . She's flooded from stem to
      stern . . .
Never seen death yet, Dickie? . . . Well, now is your time to
      learn!

A
Christmas
Cracker

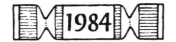

The Sunday Times, *in its issue of 13 June 1982, reported that King Fahd of Saudi Arabia had been so impressed by the Prime Minister when they met in London the previous year that he ordered his Court Poet to compose an ode in her honour. This was the result:*

Venus was sculpted by man,
But the far more attractive woman, Margaret Thatcher,
Was sculpted by Allah.
My heart raced when I saw her face to face.
Her skin was smooth as ivory,
Her cheeks as rosy as an English rose,
And her eyes as lovely as a mare's.
Her figure is more attractive than the figure of any cherished wife
Or coveted concubine.

Lytton Strachey's account, in Elizabeth and Essex, *of the death of King Philip II of Spain:*

King Philip's agony was coming to an end at last. The ravages of his dreadful diseases had overwhelmed him utterly; covered from head to foot with putrefying sores, he lay moribund in indescribable torment. His bed had been lifted into the oratory, so that his dying eyes might rest till the last moment on the high altar in the great church. He was surrounded by monks, priests, prayers, chanting and holy relics. For fifty days and nights the extraordinary scene went on. He was dying as he had lived – in absolute piety. His conscience was clear: he had always done his duty; he had been infinitely industrious; he had existed solely for virtue and the glory of God. One thought alone troubled him: had he been remiss in the burning of heretics? He had burnt many, no doubt; but he might have burnt more. Was it because of this, perhaps, that he had not been quite as successful as he might have wished? It was certainly mysterious – he could not understand it – there seemed to be something wrong with his Empire – there was never enough money – the Dutch – the Queen of England . . . as he mused, a paper was brought in. It was the dispatch from Ireland, announcing the victory of Tyrone. He sank back on his pillows, radiant; all was well, his prayers and his virtues had been rewarded, and the tide had turned at last. He dictated a letter to Tyrone of congratulation and encouragement. He promised immediate succour, he foretold the destruction of the heretics, and the ruin of the heretic Queen. A fifth Armada . . . he could dictate no more, and sank into a tortured stupor. When he awoke it was night, and there was singing at the altar below him; a sacred candle was lighted and put into his hand, the flame, as he clutched it closer and closer, casting lurid shadows upon his face; and so, in ecstasy and in torment, in absurdity and in greatness, happy, miserable, horrible, and holy, King Philip went off, to meet the Trinity.

How, one wonders, would Strachey have described the death of King Edward VII? Sir Laurence Jones, that inspired pasticheur *of a thousand* New Statesman *competitions, thought the paragraph might have run something like this:*

He was not afraid to die: had he not been punctual in attendance at Divine Service? Besides, God was known to be merciful. But in another, less placable, quarter a report would certainly be demanded. Would it be possible, there whither he was bound, to meet Papa without Mama? He must ask the Archbishop. Of some things Papa must surely approve: there had been the Entente Cordiale; there had been the Hospital Fund; there had been the Royal College of Music. No mention need be made of Minoru. And that reminded him. 'Tell Marky,' he whispered, 'I'm glad his horse won.' A few more mutterings followed, too faint to catch. Might those words have been, if caught, 'Don't let poor Cassel starve'? The words were not caught. The friendly-hearted King was dead, and the Edwardian Age, exuberant, brittle, and amusing, saw no point in surviving him.

[*Stuart Preston writes:*

I wonder how many of your readers will identify (correctly) 'Marky' as Lord Marcus Beresford, who headed the King's racing establishment.

He also suggests another possible subject of those uncaught mutterings:

The last royal victory on the turf was gained, *not* by Minoru (the 1909 Derby winner) but by Witch of the Air, who won the 4.05 race at Kempton Park on the day of the King's death. This news was conveyed to Buckingham Palace just a few hours before he sank into a final coma.]

Extracts from the Index to The Violent Effigy: A Study of Dickens'
Imagination *by John Carey:*

The church of St Mary Magdalen in the Norfolk village of Mulbarton contains a most curious memorial. It is to Mrs Sarah Scargill, who died in 1680, and it takes the form of a copper diptych resting on the wooden back of a Bible. This diptych is normally closed; it can however be opened by the winding of a handle, whereupon it reveals a poem by Mrs Scargill's husband. This runs:

Dear Love, one Feather'd minute and I come
To lye down in thy darke Retireing Roome
And mingle Dust with thine, that wee may have,
As when alive one Bed, so dead one Grave;
And may my Soul teare through the vaulted Sky
To be with thine to all Eternitie.
O how our Bloudless Formes will that Day greet
With Love Divine when we again shall meet
Devest of all Contagion of the Flesh
Fullfilled with everlasting joys and Fresh
In Heaven above (and 't may be) cast an eye
How far Elizium doth beneath us lye.

Deare, I disbody and away
More swift than Wind
Or flying Hind
I come I come away.

As a child, I used to derive much pleasure from the following advice:

If B m t, put :
If B . putting :

(If grate be empty, put coal on
If grate be full, stop putting coal on.)

Rather weak, really. A bit better was the conversation in a restaurant between a patron and the waiter, neither of them realizing that the other is also of German extraction:

F U N E X ?
S V F X .
F U N E M ?
S V F M .
O K I F M N X .

But Air Chief Marshal Sir Theodore McEvoy has shown me how much better still they do these things in France:

R I O A E T L U

(Herriot a été élu.)

or

L N N E O P Y I A V Q E I E D C D

(Hélène est née au pays grec, y a vécu et y est décédée.)

But these are still fairly elementary. Advanced students may now pass on to

J J A D I D A C K O T L A H E T D B K C D G A L E V D I
N C P I E D F I J E C O Q P D B B A J T

(Gigi a des idées assez cahotées: elle a acheté des bécasses et des geais, a élevé des hyènes, s'est payé des effigies et s'est occupée des bébés agités.)

Je voulais mourir pour elle
   Car, de toute la fête,
Elle était la plus belle —
   Et la plus bête.

Of this sad little verse I know neither the author nor the origin. It was, however, much loved by Hilaire Belloc, who used to sing it with every sign of enjoyment. Perhaps he wrote it himself.

*James Hurnand was a brewer in Colchester. He lived from 1808 to 1881
and was a compulsive poet. In 1867 he started his* magnum opus, *a poem
called 'The Setting Sun', which is divided into seven books and runs to
nearly ten thousand lines of unusually pedestrian blank verse. It could, I
suppose, be best described as a sort of rambling autobiography; and much of
it is very dull indeed. But there occasionally come, when one least expects
them, moments of curious, unanalysable charm. Here are a few:*

> Davenant was born upon the third of March,
> Waller was born upon the third of March,
> Otway was born upon the third of March,
> And I was born upon the third of March;
> But that affords no proof I am a poet.
> Thousands of blockheads in the lapse of time
> Were also born upon the third of March.
> Milton was born in sixteen hundred and eight,
> And I was born in eighteen hundred and eight;
> But what a mighty interval divides us
> Besides the simple interval of time!
>
>   *
>
> The broad High Street of good old Colchester
> May match with any street in any town,
> Ending in old East Hill – where once I dwelt,
> And which I have climbed some twenty thousand times –
> Where I brewed beer of excellent quality,
> Which I could confidently recommend
> As genuine, wholesome and invigorating,
> And thereby earned a comfortable living.
> I hope my poetry may prove as good.

It didn't; but Hurnand was used to disappointment:

> What ardour filled my soul in my young days
> For truth, for justice and for liberty . . .
> I was a humble struggler for reform;
> Wrote letters in the local newspaper
> That were attributed to some great man
> And threw my heart and soul into a poem.
> A book of doggerel Hudibrastic verse,
> Full of the grey-haired wisdom of a boy . . .
> And when at last I had completed it,
> By stealth in sweet delicious secrecy,
> And thought to rouse the very heart of England . . .
> I could not find a publisher to print it . . .
> William the IV assumed the crown of England . . .
> The iron Duke of Wellington stood up
> Among his peers, Prime Minister of England,

And uttered his immortal fulmination
Refusing all Reform in Parliament.
Then all the floodgates of the popular wrath
Were opened wide against the Ministry.
They fell – and then Earl Grey arose to power
In the year eighteen hundred thirty-one,
And with his friends carried the Whig Reform Bill . . .
The thing was done without my thunderbolt,
And done as well as if it had been fired:
A very mortifying fact indeed.

I pondered all these things, and how men fight and lose the battle, and the thing that they fought for comes about in spite of their defeat, and when it comes it turns out not to be what they meant, and other men have to fight for what they meant under another name.

William Morris

> E come il vento
> Odo stormir tra quelle piante, io quello
> Infinito silenzio a questa voce
> Vo comparando: e mi sovvien l'eterno,
> E le morte stagioni, e la presente
> E viva, e il suon di lei. Così tra questa
> Immensità s'annega il pensier mio:
> E il naufragar m'è dolce in questo mare.

This lovely passage from Leopardi might be translated:

> And as I hear
> The wind that rustles through the leaves and grass,
> So does my mind associate that voice
> With boundless silence. Then do I recall
> Eternity, the seasons that are past,
> And that which yet lives with us, and its song.
> In this immensity my thought is drowned,
> And sweet to me is shipwreck, in this sea.

[John Parker has sent me a Russian translation by Vyacheslav Ivanov:

> Слышу: ветр шуршащий
> Стронул заросль, – и сличаю в мыслях
> Ту тишину глубокого покоя
> И этот голос, – и воспомню вечность,
> И мертвые века, и время наше,
> Живущий век, и звук его . . . Так помысл
> В неизмеримости плывет – и тонет,
> И сладко мне крушенье в этом море.*]

Leopardi was three years younger than John Keats, and even more unhappy. Those last two lines always remind me of the ending of Keats's sonnet 'Bright star, would I were steadfast as thou art':

> Then on the shore
> Of the wide world I stand alone, and think
> Till love and fame to nothingness do sink.

Our long, dry summer has most forcibly reminded me of a letter to The Times *written in June 1919:*

Sir,

Observing reports in various newspapers that prayers are about to be offered up for rain in order that the present serious drought may be terminated, I venture to suggest that great care should be taken in framing the appeal.

On the last occasion when this extreme step was resorted to, the Duke of Rutland took the leading part with so much well-meaning enthusiasm that the resulting downpour was not only sufficient for all immediate needs, but was considerably in excess of what was actually required, with the consequence that the agricultural community had no sooner been delivered from the drought than they were clamouring for a special interposition to relieve them from the deluge.

Profiting from this experience, we ought surely on this occasion to be extremely careful to state exactly what we want in precise terms, so as to obviate the possibility of any misunderstanding . . . While therefore welcoming the suggestion that His Grace should again come forward, I cannot help feeling that the Board of Agriculture should first of all be consulted. They should draw up a schedule of the exact amount of rainfall required in the interests of this year's harvest in the different parts of the country. This schedule should be placarded in the various places of worship at the time when the appeal is made . . .

But, after all, even this scheme, though greatly preferable to the haphazard methods previously employed, is in itself only a partial makeshift. What we really require to pray for is the general amelioration of the British climate . . . Would it not be far better to ascertain by scientific investigation, conducted under the auspices of a Royal Commission, what is the proportion of sunshine and rain best suited to the ripening of the British crops? It would no doubt be necessary that other interests besides agriculture should be represented, but there must be certain broad general reforms in the British weather upon which an overwhelming consensus of opinion could be found . . .

These reforms, when duly embodied in an official volume, could be made the object of sustained appeals by the nation over many years, and embodied in general prayers of a permanent and not of an exceptional character. We should not then be forced from time to time to have recourse to such appeals at particular periods, which, since they are unrelated to any general plan, must

run the risk of deranging the whole economy of nature ...
causing reactions of the utmost complexity in many directions
which it is impossible for us with our limited knowledge to
foresee ...

Yours very faithfully,
SCORPIO

A carbon copy of this letter – which I have slightly abridged – was found among the papers of Sir Edward Marsh after his death. It was never printed; but one suspects that it might have been if the Editor had known the true identity of its author: Mr Winston Churchill.

In the very first Christmas Cracker I included a passage from a wonderful book to which we had recently awarded the Duff Cooper Memorial Prize. It was by J. A. Baker and was called The Peregrine. *Now, fourteen years later, I find that I cannot resist one more quotation from the same source:*

At half past two the peregrine swung up into the eastern sky. He climbed vertically upward, like a salmon leaping in the great waves of air that broke against the cliff of South Wood. He dived to the trough of a wave, then rose steeply within it, flinging himself in the air, on outstretched wings exultant. At five hundred feet he hung still, tail closed, wings curving far back with their tips almost touching the tip of his tail. He was stooping horizontally forward at the speed of the oncoming wind. He rocked and swayed and shuddered, close-hauled in a roaring sea of air, his furled wings whipping and plying like wet canvas. Suddenly he plunged to the north, curved over to the vertical stoop, flourished his wings high, shrank small, and fell.

He fell so fast, he fired so furiously from the sky to the dark wood below, that his black shape dimmed to grey air, hidden in a shining cloud of speed. He drew the sky about him as he fell. It was final. It was death. There was nothing more. Dusk came early. Through the almost dark, the fearful pigeons flew quietly down to roost above the feathered bloodstain in the woodland ride.

Compare, for no particular reason, the following passage from Peter Fleming's Brazilian Adventure:

On a branch hanging low over the water sat a kingfisher, a tiny kingfisher, a bird so small that it seemed impossible that it should exercise the functions of a kingfisher. It was smaller than a sparrow. It had a sharp black beak and sharp black eyes, surely too small to be of any service. Its markings were gay, distinct, and contrasting, like the colours of a toy. An orange chest: dark-green back and wings, very lustrous: a black head and a neat white ring round its neck. It looked very compact and proud, and at the same time rather absurd: like a medieval page in a new and splendid livery.

As I watched, it plunged suddenly, wounding the surface of the water hardly more than a falling leaf. Then it went back to the branch, having missed its prey, and sat glaring and fussing the water out of its feathers. Failure rankled. It registered a microscopic indignation.

From the second volume of Noel Coward's autobiography, Future Indefinite, *comes this description of his brief encounter with Sibelius:*

During my stay in Helsinki someone suggested that I should pay a call on Sibelius, who, although he lived a life of the utmost quiet and seclusion, would, I was assured, be more than delighted to receive me. This, later, proved to be an overstatement. However, encouraged by the mental picture of the great Master being practically unable to contain himself at the thought of meeting face to face the man who had composed 'A Room with a View' and 'Mad Dogs and Englishmen', I drove out graciously to call upon him. His house was a few miles away in the country and my guide-interpreter and I arrived there about noon. We were received by a startled, bald-headed gentleman whom I took to be an aged family retainer. He led us, without any marked signs of enthusiasm, on to a small, trellis-enclosed veranda, and left us alone. We conversed in low, reverent voices and offered each other cigarettes and waited with rising nervous tension for the Master to appear. I remember regretting bitterly my casual approach to classical music and trying frantically in my mind to disentangle the works of Sibelius from those of Delius. After about a quarter of an hour the bald-headed man reappeared carrying a tray upon which was a decanter of wine and a plate of biscuits. He put this on the table and then, to my surprise, sat down and looked at us. The silence became almost unbearable, and my friend muttered something in Finnish to which the bald-headed gentleman replied with an exasperated nod. It then dawned upon me that this was the great man himself, and furthermore that he hadn't the faintest idea who I was, who my escort was, or what we were doing there at all. Feeling embarrassed and extremely silly I smiled vacuously and offered him a cigarette, which he refused. My friend then rose, I thought a trifle officiously, and poured out three glasses of wine. We then proceeded to toast each other politely but in the same oppressive silence. I asked my friend if Mr Sibelius could speak English or French and he said 'No'. I then asked him to explain to him how very much I admired his music and what an honour it was for me to meet him personally. This was translated, upon which Sibelius rose abruptly to his feet and offered me a biscuit. I accepted it with rather overdone gratitude, and then down came the silence again, and I looked forlornly past Sibelius's head through a gap in the trellis at the road. Finally, realising that unless I did something decisive we should probably stay there until sundown, I got up and asked my friend – whom I could willingly have garrotted –to thank Mr Sibelius for receiving me and to explain once again how honoured I was to meet him, and that I hoped he would forgive us for leaving so soon but we had an appointment at the hotel for lunch. Upon this being communicated to him, Sibelius smiled for the first time and we shook hands with enthusiasm. He escorted us to the gate and waved happily as we drove away.

When first her love began on me to shine
It pleased her to call me Valentine –
But since her loves to mee decreasèd dayly
Nothing is left of Valentine but Vale.

From a Bodleian MS
Ashmole 47, 56v

That the great Angell-blinding light should shrinke
His blaze, to shine in a poor shepherd's eye;
That the unmeasured God so low should sinke
As pris'ner in a few poore Rags to lye.
That from His Mother's breast He milke should drinke
Who feeds with Nectar Heav'n's faire family;
    That a vile Manger His low Bed should prove
    Who in a Throne of stars thunders above.

That He whom the sun serves should faintly peep
Through clouds of infant flesh; that He, the old
Eternall Worde should be a Child, and weep;
That He who made the fire should fear the cold,
That Heav'n's high Majesty His court should keepe
In a clay cottage, by each blast controll'd;
    That Glorie's self should serve our griefs and fears,
    And free Eternity submit to yeares.

Richard Crashaw
(1612?–49)

*Mr Kevin Brownlow has kindly sent me the full text of the appeal made by
the film director Abel Gance to all the 'artists, technicians and extras'
engaged for work on his magnificent silent epic* Napoleon. *Most of the
extras were in fact workers from the Renault factory who, at that crucial
moment in 1926, happily chanced to be on strike. The appeal was posted on
the main door of Gance's studios at Billancourt, and runs as follows:*

Il faut, entendez bien le sens profond que je mets dans ces mots,
il faut que ce film nous permette d'entrer définitivement dans le
temple des arts par la gigantesque porte de l'Histoire. Une
angoisse indicible m'étreint à la pensée que ma volonté et le don
de ma vie même ne sont rien si vous ne m'apportez pas tous un
dévouement de toutes les secondes. Nous allons, grâce à vous,
revivre la Révolution et l'Empire. La tâche est inouïe. Il faut
retrouver en vous la flamme, la folie, la puissance des soldats de
l'An II. L' initiative personelle va compter. Je veux sentir en vous
contemplant une houle de force qui puisse emporter toutes les
digues du sens critique, de façon que je ne distingue plus de loin
entre vos coeurs et vos bonnets rouges. Rapides, fous, tumultueux,
gigantesques, gouailleurs, homériques, avec des pauses, des points
d'orgue qui rendent les silences plus redoutables: ainsi vous veut
la Révolution, cette cavalle emballée. Et puis un homme qui la
regarde en face, qui la comprend, qui veut s'en servir pour le bien
de la France et qui brusquement saut sur elle, la saisit par les
rênes et peu à peu l'apaise pour en faire le plus miraculeux
instrument de gloire. La Révolution et son rire d'agonie, l'Empire
et ses ombres géantes, la Grande Armée et ses soleils, c'est à vous
qu'il incombe d'en recréer les immortelles figures. Mes amis, tous
les écrans de l'univers vous attendent. A tous, collaborateurs de
tous ordres, premiers rôles, seconds plans, opérateurs, peintres,
électriciens, machinistes, à tous, surtout à vous, humbles figurants
qui allez avoir le lourd fardeau de retrouver l'esprit de vos aïeux
et de donner par votre unité de coeur le redoutable visage de la
France de 1792 à 1815, je demande, mieux, j'exige l'oubli total
des mesquines considérations personelles et un dévouement
absolu. Ainsi seulement vous servirez pieusement la cause déjà
illustre du plus bel art de l'avenir à travers la plus merveilleuse
des leçons de l'histoire!

*As Mr Brownlow has noted, the Renault management had never talked
to their workers quite like that.*

God in the whizzing of a pleasant wind
Shall march upon the tops of mulberry trees.

George Peele
(1558?–98)

See I Chronicles xiv:15.

Looking through the pile of former Crackers, I note with some surprise that it is five years since we had any Pepys. Here are two entries. The first is dated 3 November 1661:

Lord's Day. This day I stirred not out, but took physique and it did work very well; and all the day, as I was at leisure, I did read in Fuller's *Holy Warr* (which I have of late bought) and did try to make a Song in the prayse of a Liberall genius (as I take my own to be) to all studies and pleasures; but it not proving to my mind, I did reject it and so proceeded not in it. At night my wife and I had a good supper by ourselfs, of a pullet-hashed; which pleased me much to see my condition come to allow ourselfs a dish like that. And so at night to bed.

In his entry for 15 December 1662, Pepys casts an unexpected light on the Duke of York – the future King James II:

Up and to my Lord's [Lord Sandwich] and thence to the Duke and followed him into the parke [St James's]; where though the ice was broken and dangerous, yet he would go slide upon his Scates; which I did not like, but he slides very well.

Thomas Fuller (1608–61) whose History of the Holy Warr – *i.e. the* Crusades – *kept Pepys company through his day of leisure, is probably better known for his* Church History *and his great unfinished* Worthies of England. *He was once described, by Dr Robert South in the course of a public oration at Oxford, as 'running around London with his big book under one arm and his little wife under the other'. He does indeed seem to have been something of a snob, and he certainly knew how to trim his sails – a vital necessity for any prominent churchman of royalist tendencies who wished to survive the Civil War and the Commonwealth. But he talked as entertainingly as he wrote, and when he preached he is said always to have had two congregations, 'one in the church, the other listening through the windows'. Somewhere – I stupidly forgot to note the source – he writes:*

I saw a servant-maid, at the command of her mistress, make, kindle and blow a fire. Which done, she was posted away about other business, whilst her mistress enjoyed the benefit of the fire. Yet I observed that this servant, whilst industriously employed in the kindling thereof, got a more general, kindly, and continuing heat than her mistress herself. Her heat was only by her, and not in her, staying with her no longer than she stayed by the chimney; whilst the warmth of the maid was inlaid, and equally diffused through the whole body.

Elsewhere, he notes:

A man ought to be like a cunning actor, who if he be enjoined to represent the person of some prince or nobleman, does it with a grace and comeliness; if, by and by, he be commanded to lay that aside and play the beggar, he does that as willingly and as well.

That made the buggers hop.

Sir Thomas Beecham, after conducting the Dance of the Cygnets (from Swan Lake) for the ballet of the Camargo Society at about twice the normal speed.

One time, however, we were near quarrelling. He said the pleasantest manner of spending a hot July day was lying from morning till evening on a bank of heath in the middle of the moors, with the bees humming dreamily about among the bloom, and the larks singing high up overhead, and the blue sky and bright sun shining steadily and cloudlessly. This was his most perfect idea of heaven's happiness. Mine was rocking in a rustling green tree, with a west wind blowing, and bright white clouds flitting rapidly above, and not only larks, but throstles, and blackbirds, and linnets, and cuckoos pouring out music on every side, and the moors seen at a distance, broken into cool, dusky dells, but close by great swells of long grass undulating in waves to the breeze, and woods and sounding water, and the whole world awake and wild with joy. He wanted to lie in an ecstasy of peace; I wanted all to sparkle and dance in a glorious jubilee. I said his heaven would be only half alive, and he said mine would be drunk; I said I should fall asleep in his, and he said he could not breathe in mine, and began to grow very snappish. At last we agreed to try both, as soon as the right weather came; and then we kissed each other and were friends.

Emily Brontë
Wuthering Heights

'Where are you, Adam?'
  'I'm behind this tree, Lord.'

'What are you doing there?'
  'Nothing, Lord. I'm naked is all.'

'Who told you you were naked?'
  'I noticed it, Lord.'

'Naked, schmaked, what does it matter?'
  'You can get six months for indecency, Lord.'

'What's six months to you, you're immortal.'
  'It might give the animals funny thoughts.'

'My animals don't have funny thoughts.'
  'The best people wear suits, Lord.'

'You were the best people, Adam.'
  'The weather might change, Lord.'

'Too right. It will.'

D. J. Enright
Paradise Illustrated

This quotation appears on the last page of David Newsome's fascinating biography of A. C. Benson, On the Edge of Paradise. *It is said to have been written on the title page of the Duchess of Sutherland's keepsake. I wish I knew where it came from.*

'Let me take your hand for love, and sing you a song,' said the other traveller. 'The journey is a hard journey, but if we hold together in the morning and in the evening, what matter if in the hours between there is sorrow?'

I found the following in Auden and MacNeice's Letters from Iceland – *essential reading for anyone lucky enough to visit that astonishing country. On my first visit in 1974, to while away long hours trundling from coast to coast in a bus, I learnt it by heart; it has stayed with me ever since. The authors do not reveal which of them wrote the poem, but all the evidence points to Auden.*

'Oh who can ever gaze his fill,'
   Farmer and fisherman say,
'On native shore and local hill,
Grudge aching limb or callous on the hand?
Fathers, grandfathers stood upon this land,
And here the pilgrims from our loins shall stand.'
   So farmer and fisherman say
   In their fortunate heyday:
   But Death's soft answer drifts across
   Empty catch or harvest loss
    Or an unlucky May.

The earth is an oyster with nothing inside it
   Not to be born is the best for man
The end of toil is a bailiff's order
   Throw down the mattock and dance while you can.

'Oh life's too short for friends who share,'
   Travellers think in their hearts,
'The city's common bed, the air,
The mountain bivouac and the bathing beach,
Where incidents draw every day from each
Memorable gesture and witty speech.'
   So travellers think in their hearts,
   Till malice or circumstance parts
   Them from their constant humour:
   And shyly Death's coercive rumour
    In the silence starts.

A friend is the old, old tale of Narcissus
   Not to be born is the best for man
An active partner is something disgraceful
   Change your partner, dance while you can.

'Oh stretch your hands across the sea,'
   The impassioned lover cries,
'Stretch them towards your harm and me.
Our grass is green, and sensual our brief bed,
The stream sings at its foot, and at its head

The mild and vegetarian beasts are fed.'
　　So the impassioned lover cries
　　Till his storm of pleasure dies:
　　From the bedpost and the rocks
　　Death's enticing echo mocks
　　　And his voice replies.

The greater the love, the more false to its object
　　Not to be born is the best for man
After the kiss comes the impulse to throttle
　　Break the embraces, dance while you can.

'I see the guilty world forgiven,'
　　Dreamer and drunkard sing,
'The ladders let down out of heaven;
The laurel springing from the martyrs' blood;
The children skipping where the weepers stood;
The lovers natural, and the beasts all good.'
　　So dreamer and drunkard sing
　　Till day their sobriety bring:
　　Parrotwise with Death's reply
　　From whelping fear and nesting lie
　　　Woods and their echoes ring.

The desires of the heart are as crooked as corkscrews
　　Not to be born is the best for man
The second best is a formal order
　　The dance's pattern, dance while you can.
Dance, dance, for the figure is easy
　　The tune is catching and will not stop
Dance till the stars come down with the rafters
　　Dance, dance, dance till you drop.

A
Christmas
Cracker

|1985|

Apart from the fact that they prostitute their daughters, the Lydian way of life is not unlike our own.

Herodotus

The 1981 Cracker included [p. 53] a poem by George Peele, 'A Farewell to Arms', of which the second verse began with the line

His helmet now shall make a hive for bees.

My friend John Yeoman, on reading it, immediately called my attention to another poem which, he pointed out, had an almost identical first line. Its author is a little-known poet named Ralph Knevet, who lived from 1600 to 1671 and was for some twenty years Rector of Lyng, in Norfolk. Despite the surface similarities, the two poems are very different in mood. Peele's is essentially about old age, full of nostalgia for battles long ago; Knevet's is, quite simply, a paean to peace – written, presumably, soon after the end of the Civil War. It runs like this:

> The helmet now a hive for bees becomes,
> And hilts of swords may serve for spiders' looms;
> > Sharp pikes may make
> > Teeth for a rake;
> And the keen blade, th' arch enemy of life
> Shall be degraded to a pruning knife.
> > The rustic spade
> > Which first was made
> For honest agriculture, shall retake
> Its primitive employment, and forsake
> > The rampires steep
> > And trenches deep.
> Tame conies in our brazen guns shall breed,
> Or gentle doves their young ones there shall feed.
> > In musket barrels
> > Mice shall raise quarrels
> For their quarters. The ventriloquious drum,
> Like lawyers in vacations, shall be dumb.
> > Now all recruits,
> > But those of fruits,
> Shall be forgot; and th' unarmed soldier
> Shall only boast of what he did whilere,
> > In chimneys' ends
> > Among his friends.

Upon the same River [the Gipping] are seene two little Mercat Townes, *Stow* and *Needham*, and not farre from the banke, *Hemingston*: in which *Baldwin Le Petteur* (marke his name well) helde certaine lands, by Serjeanty, (the words I have out of an old booke) for which on Christmasse day, every yeere before our soveraigne Lord the King of England he should performe one *Saltus*, one *Suffletus*, and one *Bumbulus*, or, as wee read elsewhere, his tenour was, *per saltum, sufflum, & pettum*, that is, if I understand these tearmes aright, *That hee should daunce, puffe up his cheekes making therewith a sound, and besides let a cracke downeward*. Such was the plaine and jolly mirth of those times.

Just ten years ago, in the 1975 Cracker, I quoted two of my favourite book dedications. It is time we had some more. From Richard Ellmann's superb biography of James Joyce I learn that Joyce, when still only eighteen, wrote a play. It was called A Brilliant Career, *and*

... with due sense of its importance and his own, [he] inscribed on the dedicatory page:

To
My own Soul I
dedicate the first
true work of my
life.

It was the only work he was ever to dedicate to anyone.

Another curious dedication can be found in the volume covering London 2: South *in Dr Pevsner's majestic* The Buildings of England *series. The title page bears, as well as the name of Nikolaus Pevsner, that of Bridget Cherry, and the dedication is hers. It runs:*

To the Marshes
Of Clapham, Balham and Tooting.

But the good doctor himself is no slouch in this field. His volume on Yorkshire: The North Riding *bears the dedication:*

To those Publicans
and Hoteliers of England
who provide me with a table
in my bedroom to
scribble on

and that on Bedfordshire and the County of Huntingdonshire and Peterborough

To the
Inventor
of the
ICED LOLLY

One of the buildings about which Dr Pevsner was scribbling on his bedroom table was All Saints' Church at Foston-le-Clay, where the Rev. Sydney Smith was parson from 1806 to 1829. He described it thus:

My living in Yorkshire was so far out of the way that it was actually twelve miles from a lemon. I have no relish for country life; it is a kind of healthy grave. In the country, one always feels that creation may expire before tea-time.

Smith was the first incumbent for over a century. As he later recalled:

When I began to thump the pulpit cushion on my first coming to Foston, the accumulated dust of 150 years made such a cloud that for some minutes I lost sight of my congregation.

Another memorable remark from the same source:

I had a wonderful dream last night. I dreamed that there were thirty-nine Muses and only nine articles.

'As you came from the holy land
  Of Walsingham,
Met you not with my true love
  By the way as you came?'
'How shall I know your true love,
  That have met many one
As I went to the holy land,
  That have come, that have gone?'
'She is neither white nor brown,
  But as the heavens fair,
There is none hath a form so divine
  In the earth or the air.'
'Such an one did I meet, good Sir,
  Such an angelic face,
Who like a queen, like a nymph did appear
  By her gait, by her grace.'
'She hath left me here all alone,
  All alone as unknown,
Who sometimes did me lead with herself,
  And me loved as her own.'
'What's the cause that she leaves you alone
  And a new way doth take,
Who loved you once as her own
  And her joy did you make?'
'I have loved her all my youth,
  But now as you see,
Love likes not the falling fruit
  From the withered tree.
'Know that love is a careless child,
  And forgets promise past;
He is blind, he is deaf when he list
  And in faith never fast.
'His desire is a dureless content
  And a trustless joy;
He is won with a world of despair
  And is lost with a toy.'
'Of womenkind such indeed is the love
  Or the word love abused,
Under which many childish desires
  And conceits are excused.
'But true Love is a durable fire
  In the mind ever burning;
Never sick, never old, never dead,
  From itself never turning.'

Sir Walter Ralegh

On 2 September 1870, following his catastrophic defeat at Sedan, Napoleon III saw that he had no choice but surrender. In his book The Franco-Prussian War, *Michael Howard quotes the exchange of letters that followed between the Emperor and the King of Prussia. The first letter Professor Howard describes as 'not the least of the title-deeds of the Second German Reich'. It ran:*

Monsieur mon frère,

N'ayant pas pu mourir au milieu de mes troupes, il ne me reste qu' à remettre mon épée entre les mains de Votre Majesté. Je suis de Votre Majesté le bon frère.

Napoléon.

The reply was dictated by Bismarck himself:

Monsieur mon frère,

En regrettant les circonstances dans lesquelles nous nous rencontrons, j'accepte l'épée de Votre Majesté et je la prie de vouloir bien nommer un de vos officiers muni de vos pleins pouvoirs pour traiter de la capitulation de l'armée, qui s'est si bravement battue sous vos ordres. De mon côté, j'ai désigné le Général de Moltke à cet effet.

Wilhelm.

If there is honour among thieves, so also there is – or was – politeness among highwaymen. In an unsigned article published in the World *on 19 December 1754, Horace Walpole told – rather succinctly, for him – how he had had a narrow escape in the park some years before:*

> One night in the beginning of November 1749 as I was returning from Holland House by moonlight, about ten at night, I was attacked by two highwaymen in Hyde Park, and the pistol of one of them, going off accidentally, razed the skin under my eye, left some marks of shot on my face, and stunned me. The ball went through the top of the chariot, and if I had sat an inch nearer to the left side, must have gone through my head.

Note in particular the word 'accidentally'. At the time, it appears, Walpole had not been too sure whether the explosion had been an accident or not – until, a few days after his adventure, he received two letters of excuses which, he wrote to a friend, 'with less wit than the epistles of Voltaire, had ten times more natural and easy politeness in the turn of their expression'. One of them read as follows:

Sir,

> Seeing an advertisement in the papers of to Day giveing an account of your being Rob'd by two Highway men on wednesday night last in Hyde Parke and during the time a Pistol being fired whether Intended or Accidentally was Doubtfull Oblidges us to take this Method of assureing you that it was the latter and by no means Design'd Either to hurt or frighten you.

The letter was written – though not, I think, actually signed – by the famous James Maclean (or, as he was sometimes called, Maclaine). He was known as the 'gentleman highwayman', being the son of a Scottish Presbyterian minister and brother of the equally famous divine Alexander Maclean, translator of Mosheim's Ecclesiastical History. *In the other letter he offered to sell back to Walpole any trifles he might want, and suggested meeting him at Tyburn at midnight. Walpole did not accept – possibly the time and place proposed had something to do with it – but when in the following year Maclean was captured and put on trial, he refused to testify against him. Alas, Maclean was hanged all the same – at Tyburn on 3 October 1750. He was twenty-five years old.*

And, talking of highwaymen, I cannot resist transcribing the epitaph of another. This was the Frenchman Claude du Vall, who was hanged (like Maclean) at Tyburn, but nearly a century earlier – on 21 January 1670, aged twenty-seven. He was outstandingly handsome, and had a success with women approaching the legendary: indeed, he has a good claim to be one of the first examples in history of radical chic. After his death, his admirers gave him a magnificent funeral at St Paul's, Covent Garden, and inscribed on his tombstone the following words:

Here lies Du Vall: Reader, if Male thou art,
Look to thy Purse; if Female, to thy heart.
Much havoc has he made of both; for all
Men he made stand, and women he made fall.
The second Conqueror of the Norman race,
Knights to his arms did yield, and Ladies to his face.
Old Tyburn's glory; England's illustrious thief,
Du Vall, the Ladies' joy; Du Vall, the Ladies' grief.

There is hardly anything in the world that some man cannot make a little worse and sell a little cheaper, and the people who consider price only are this man's lawful prey.

Ruskin

As I write these words, the fate of the luckless hostages held captive in Beirut airport still hangs in the balance; and it seems to me, in these days of hijackings, kidnappings and all the other fashionable forms of blackmail, that a certain poem of Kipling's should be a good deal better known than it is. It goes like this:

DANE-GELD
AD 980–1016

It is always a temptation to an armed and agile nation,
    To call upon a neighbour and to say:–
'We invaded you last night – we are quite prepared to fight,
    Unless you pay us cash to go away.'

    And that is called asking for Dane-geld,
        And the people who ask it explain
    That you've only to pay 'em the Dane-geld
        And then you'll get rid of the Dane!

It is always a temptation to a rich and lazy nation,
    To puff and look important and to say:–
'Though we know we should defeat you, we have not
        the time to meet you,
    We will therefore pay you cash to go away.'

    And that is called paying the Dane-geld,
        But we've proved it again and again,
    That if once you have paid him the Dane-geld
        You'll never get rid of the Dane.

It is wrong to put temptation in the path of any nation,
    For fear they should succumb and go astray;
So when you are requested to pay up or be molested,
    You will find it better policy to say:–

    'We never pay anyone Dane-geld,
        No matter how trifling the cost;
    For the end of that game is oppression and shame,
        And the nation that plays it is lost!'

On the day I first sat down with Johnson, in his rusty brown, and his black worsteds, Gibbon was placed opposite to me in a suit of flower'd velvet, with a bag and sword. Each had his measured phraseology; and Johnson's famous parallel between Dryden and Pope might be loosely parodied, in reference to himself and Gibbon. Johnson's style was grand, and Gibbon's elegant; the stateliness of the former was sometimes pedantick, and the polish of the latter was occasionally finical. Johnson march'd to kettle-drums and trumpets; Gibbon moved to flutes and hautboys; Johnson hew'd passages through the Alps, while Gibbon levell'd walks through parks and gardens. Maul'd as I had been by Johnson, Gibbon pour'd balm upon my bruises, by condescend-ing, once or twice, in the course of the evening, to talk with me; the great historian was light and playful, suiting his matter to the capacity of the boy; – but it was done *more suo*; still his mannerisms prevail'd; – still he tapp'd his snuff-box, – still he smurk'd, and smiled; and rounded his periods with the same air of good-breeding, as if he were conversing with men. His mouth, melliflu-ous as Plato's, was a round hole, nearly in the centre of his visage.

So wrote the playwright George Colman the younger, in Random Records; *and how one would love to have been at* that *gathering! As for 'Johnson's famous parallel', it was recorded by Boswell as follows:*

I told him that Voltaire, in a conversation with me, had distin-guished Pope and Dryden thus:– 'Pope drives a handsome chariot with a couple of neat trim nags, Dryden a coach, and six stately horses!' JOHNSON: 'Why, Sir, the truth is, they both drive coaches and six, but Dryden's horses are either galloping or stumbling; Pope's go at a steady, even trot.'

Pope idolized Dryden, and never forgot having once as a boy been taken to see him, holding court at Will's coffee house. In 1711 he wrote to his friend John Caryll:

I keep pictures of Dryden, Milton, Shakespeare, &c., in my chamber, round about me, that the constant remembrance of 'em may keep me always humble.

(A pity we cannot hear Dryden on Pope, but as the former died when the latter was twelve we are hardly likely to do so this side of eternity.)

My own favourite criticism of Dryden is Macaulay's:

His mind was of a slovenly character, – fond of splendour, but indifferent to neatness. Hence most of his writings exhibit the sluttish magnificence of a Russian noble, all vermin, diamonds, dirty linen and inestimable sables.

No, we cannot hear Dryden on Pope; but we can hear Edith Sitwell, who wrote his biography:

Even if they try to speak to him kindly, their language is one that is unknown to him. He must suffer within his heart the mad tempests of love for the world of sight, sense and sound, and the mad tempests of rage against the cruelty and blindness that there is in the world. But he must suffer these dumbly, for among the tall strangers there is nothing but noise and buffeting. The children are terrifying to him; their eyes are on a level with his own, but they are like the blind and beautiful eyes of statues – they see nothing. He loves them and longs to be loved in return, but he knows that they, too, see him as a statue throwing some long, strange shadow, or as a little foreigner dressed in mourning for someone they have never known, or playing an unknown game he has learned in far-off gardens.

Is she, I wonder, writing as much of herself as of him?

Clément Marot was the favourite poet of Mary Queen of Scots; in 1520 he accompanied François I to the Field of the Cloth of Gold. He was in fact the Renaissance court poet par excellence, *and his verses tend to be memorable more for their technical virtuosity than for any real depth of feeling. Charm, however, he possesses in abundance. Try this:*

DE SOY MESME

Plus ne suis ce que j'ay esté,
Et ne le sçaurois jamais estre;
Mon beau printemps et mon esté
Ont fait le sault par la fenestre.
Amour, tu as esté mon maistre:
Je t'ai servi sur tous les dieux.
O si je pouvais deux fois naistre,
Comme je te servirois mieux!

Last summer I tried to translate it. The result is, inevitably, a fairly free translation – apart from anything else, there are no rhymes for 'window' – but it captures, I like to think, something of the spirit of the original:

I am no longer what I was,
And never can be, never more;
My spring and summer both, alas,
Have bolted out the stable door.
I served you, Love, with might and main,
Above all gods, for good and ill;
And could I but be born again,
O love, I'd serve you better still.

Here is Virginia Woolf, confiding to her diary on 18 September 1918 her impressions of Sidney and Beatrice Webb:

I wonder how I can recapture the curious discomfort of soul which Mrs Webb produces each time I see her again? . . . There's something absolutely unadorned and impersonal about her. She makes one feel insignificant, and a little out of key.

We sat down to tea . . . They eat quickly and efficiently and leave me with hunks of cake on my hands . . . Mrs Webb rapidly gave me her reasons for saying that she had never met a great man, or woman either. At most, she said, they possessed remarkable single qualities, but looked at as a whole there was no greatness in them. Shakespeare she did not appreciate, because a sister, who was a foolish woman, always quoted him wrong to her as a child. Goethe might conceivably have been a great man . . .

After dinner Mrs Webb plunged from brisk argument to unconcealed snoring. Then Sidney had his turn. I thought he spoke a little quick to conceal the snores, but you have only to ask him a question and he can go on informing you till you can hold no more. He sketched his idea of a Supernational authority and the future of Bills of Exchange. The work of Government will be enormously increased in the future. I asked whether I should ever have a finger in the pie? 'Oh yes, you will have some small office no doubt. My wife and I always say that a Railway Guard is the most enviable of men. He has authority, and he is responsible to a Government. That should be the state of each one of us . . .'

I asked (in reporting conversations one's own sayings stand out like lighthouses) one of my most fruitful questions, viz; how easy is it for a man to change his social grade? This brought down a whole shower-bath of information, but let us say that the Webbs' shower-baths are made of soda-water. They never sink one, or satiate. Webb told us how many scholarships were won in London in a given year, and also reported upon the educational system of E. Sussex, which bad though it is, is slightly better than that of W. Sussex . . .

Next day . . . the downs were at their best; and set Mrs W. off upon landscape beauty, and recollections of India . . . Sidney, one perceives, has no organ of sight whatever, and pretends to none. Mrs W. has a compartment devoted to nature. So briskly relating their travels and impressions, which were without respect for British rule, they set off home. I saw them from behind, a shabby, homely, dowdy couple, marching with the uncertain step of strength just beginning to fail, she clutching his arm, and looking much older than he, in her angularity. They were like pictures in French papers of English tourists, only wanting spectacles and Baedekers to finish them.

In The Oxford Book of Oxford, *Jan Morris quotes the English translation of a Latin epitaph in the cloisters of Winchester College:*

Beneath this Marble is Buried
Tho. Welsted
Who was Struck Down by the Throwing of a Stone.
He was First in this School
And we Hope is not Last in Heaven
Whither he went
Instead of to Oxford
January 13, 1676
Aged 18.

Some time ago, when in Winchester, I looked for this inscription and, failing to find it, wrote in despair to the Captain of the School to ask his help. In a charming reply, he told me that he had never before heard of the existence of such a memorial, but that he had eventually discovered it 'in an obscure corner of the Old Cloisters, that are next to the Chapel'. The Latin text runs:

Hoc sub marmore sepultus est
Tho. Welsted
quem calculi ictu mors
prostravit in hac schola
primus erat nec
ut speramus in caelo ultimus est
quod pro Oxonio adiit
13 die Ianuarii

Anno Domini 1676
aetatis suae 18.

On bringing up children:

You may give them your love
But not your thoughts,
For they have their own thoughts.

You may house their bodies
But not their souls
For their souls dwell in the house of tomorrow.

You may strive to be like them
But seek not to make them like you.

For life goes not backward
Nor tarries with yesterday.

Persian poet
Third century AD

[Persian poet my foot: the lines turn out to be by the twentieth-century Lebanese mystic Khalil Gibran. Had I known at the time I should never have included them; but there they are, and there they must stay.]

The history of the papacy in the ninth and tenth centuries is not altogether edifying. Even if we discount the story of the Englishwoman Pope Joan (who, so the legend goes, managed to conceal her sex throughout her three-year pontificate until, by some unhappy miscalculation, she gave birth to a baby on the steps of the Lateran) we are left with several other pontiffs, indisputably real, whose stories are scarcely less fantastic: John VIII, for example, hammered to death by his jealous relations; Formosus, whose dead body was exhumed, brought to trial before a synod of bishops, stripped, mutilated and cast into the Tiber, then miraculously recovered, rehabilitated and reinterred in its former tomb; or John X, strangled in the Castel Sant' Angelo by his mistress's daughter so that she could instal on the papal throne her own bastard son by Pope Sergius III. Nobody, I suspect, enjoyed writing about the papal 'pornocracy' more than Edward Gibbon. Here he is on Pope John XII:

> The influence of two sister prostitutes, Marozia and Theodora, was founded on their wealth and beauty, their political and amorous intrigues: the most strenuous of their lovers were rewarded with the Roman mitre, and their reign may have suggested to the darker ages the fable of a female Pope. The bastard son, the grandson and the great-grandson of Marozia, a rare genealogy, were seated in the chair of St Peter; and it was at the age of nineteen years that the second of these became the head of the Latin church. His youth and manhood were of a suitable complexion; and the nations of pilgrims could bear testimony to the charges that were urged against him in a Roman synod, and in the presence of Otho the Great. As John XII had renounced the dress and decencies of his profession, the *soldier* may not perhaps be dishonoured by the wine which he drank, the blood that he spilt, the flames that he kindled, or the licentious pursuits of gaming and hunting. His open simony might be the consequence of distress; and his blasphemous invocation of Jupiter and Venus, if it be true, could not possibly be serious. But we read, with some surprise, that the worthy grandson of Marozia lived in public adultery with the matrons of Rome; that the Lateran Palace was turned into a school for prostitution; and that his rapes of virgins and widows had deterred the female pilgrims from visiting the tomb of St Peter, lest, in the devout act, they should be violated by his successor.

Of Gibbon, his contemporary Richard Porson (who became Regius Professor of Greek at Cambridge) wrote:

> His reflections are often just and profound; he pleads eloquently for the rights of mankind, and the duty of toleration; nor does his humanity ever slumber, unless when women are ravished, or the Christians persecuted.

On 20 September 1586 a young English Catholic, Chideock Tichborne, was hanged in the Tower for having been implicated in the Babington Plot to assassinate Queen Elizabeth and to put Mary Queen of Scots on the throne. The night before his execution, he wrote this poem:

My prime of youth is but a frost of cares,
   My feast of joy is but a dish of pain,
My crop of corn is but a field of tares,
   And all my goodes is but vain hope of gain.
The day is fled, and yet I saw no sun,
And now I live, and now my life is done!

My spring is past, and yet it has not sprung,
   The fruit is dead, and yet the leaves are green,
My youth is past, and yet I am but young,
   I saw the world, and yet I was not seen;
My thread is cut, and yet it is not spun,
And now I live, and now my life is done!

I sought for death, and found it in the wombe,
   I lookt for life, and yet it was a shade,   .
I trode the ground, and knew it was my tombe,
   And now I dye, and now I am but made,
The glass is full, and yet my glass is run;
And now I live, and now my life is done!

Twenty-eight years old when he died, he suffered – according to the Dictionary of National Biography *– 'the full penalty of the law, being disembowelled before life was extinct. The news of these barbarities reached the ears of Elizabeth, who forbade their recurrence.'*

A few years ago my old friends Lennox and Freda Berkeley passed on to me the programme of a gala performance by the National Ballet of Senegal. Here is a slightly shortened version:

Part I

Balante: It's the first hunting part of the young balante initiates, scarcely left the division of the brain. Going back the village, celebrated by their promises, they fastly recover the lofty self respect and the harmony of circumcision steps.

Silimbo or the three phases of the circumcision in mandinguo and diola country.

1. The village paves the way for the future initiates.

2. The young in circumcision have been brought up in the sacred forest by the masters of initiation.

3. The village celebrates the exit of the young initiates.

Part II

By herself, the orphan hopeless BINTA has only a weak and selfish father, unable to give her slightest pull. Left to surly and hate of an unrighteous and jaleous stepmother, who doesn't dispossess to have her suffered, she has to wash a small dirty spoon to meet without slightest chance of success cosmic shears of the bush, and her triumphal going back will confirm the existence of an immanent justice more than all stepmothers of the world and which protects weak and infortunate persons against wicked persons.

Penda, a pampered girl, unconscious and irresponsible because protected by the mother, will die to defy nature's shears veneration of which has been based on whole african mystic then all its civilisation.

From James Agate's Ego, *September 27 1933:*

Supper at Café Royal with A. P. Herbert, his wife, and Peacock,
Golding Bright's partner, a fanatical Proustian who was extremely
interested in the identity of Albertine and in how, at Albert's
hotel, I once saw the coat-tails of the master followed by a boy
carrying a cage of white mice and some hat-pins.

I wish Nelson would stop signalling. We all know well enough what to do.

Admiral Collingwood
Trafalgar, 21 October 1805

*Fauré's settings of Verlaine have always seemed to me almost too beautiful,
seducing one to the point where one forgets to listen to the magic of the
words themselves. My favourite of them all is 'Clair de Lune', a perfect
evocation of that misty, melancholic Watteau-world that Verlaine recreated
and made his own:*

Votre âme est un paysage choisi
Que vont charmant masques et bergamasques,
Jouant du luth, et dansant, et quasi
Tristes sous leurs déguisements fantasques.

Tout en chantant sur le mode mineur
L'amour vainqueur et la vie opportune,
Ils n'ont pas l'air de croire à leur bonheur
Et leur chanson se mêle au clair de lune.

Au calme clair de lune triste et beau,
Qui fait rêver les oiseaux dans les arbres
Et sangloter d'extase les jets d'eau,
Les grands jets d'eau sveltes parmi les marbres.

Thyself away are present still with me;
For thou not further than my thoughts canst move,
And I am still with them, and they with thee . . .

Shakespeare
Sonnet XXX

Of all the poems ever written about Venice, the best by far – infinitely better than anything Byron ever managed – seems to me to be Browning's 'A Toccata of Galuppi's'. The fact that Baldassare (or Baldassaro) Galuppi never wrote a Toccata in his life is immaterial: what matters is the almost uncanny way in which the poet has caught the spirit of eighteenth-century Venice:

I

Oh Galuppi, Baldassaro, this is very sad to find!
I can hardly misconceive you; it would prove me deaf and blind;
But although I take your meaning, 'tis with such a heavy mind!

II

Here you come with your old music, and here's all the good it
    brings.
What, they lived once thus at Venice where the merchants were
    the kings,
Where St Mark's is, where the Doges used to wed the sea with
    rings?

III

Ay, because the sea's the street there; and 'tis arched by . . .
    what you call
. . . Shylock's bridge with houses on it, where they kept the
    carnival:
I was never out of England – it's as if I saw it all.

IV

Did young people take their pleasure when the sea was warm in
    May?
Balls and masks begun at midnight, burning ever to mid-day,
When they made up fresh adventures for the morrow, do you
    say?

V

Was a lady such a lady, cheeks so round and lips so red, –
On her neck the small face buoyant, like a bell-flower on its bed,
O'er the breast's superb abundance where a man might base his
    head?

VI

Well, and it was graceful of them – they'd break talk off and
    afford
– She, to bite her mask's black velvet – he, to finger on his
    sword,
While you sat and played Toccatas, stately at the clavichord.

VII

What? Those lesser thirds so plaintive, sixths diminished, sigh
    on sigh,
Told them something? Those suspensions, those solutions –
    'Must we die?'
Those commiserating sevenths – 'Life might last! we can but
    try!'

VIII

'Were you happy?' – 'Yes.' – 'And are you still as happy?' –
    'Yes. And you?'
Then, more kisses! – Did I stop them, when a million seemed
    so few?
Hark, the dominant's persistence till it must be answered to!

IX

So, an octave struck the answer. Oh, they praised you, I dare
    say!
'Brave Galuppi! that was music! good alike at grave and gay!
I can always leave off talking when I hear a master play!'

X

Then they left you for their pleasure: till in due time, one by
    one,
Some with lives that came to nothing, some with deeds as well
    undone,
Death stepped tacitly and took them where they never see the
    sun.

XI

But when I sit down to reason, think to take my stand nor
    swerve,
While I triumph o'er a secret wrung from nature's close
    reserve,
In you come with your cold music till I creep thro' every
    nerve.

XII

Yes, you, like a ghostly cricket, creaking where a house was
    burned:
'Dust and ashes, dead and done with, Venice spent what Venice
    earned.
The soul, doubtless, is immortal – where a soul can be
    discerned.

XIII

'Yours for instance: you know physics, something of geology,
Mathematics are your pastime; souls shall rise in their degree;
Butterflies may dread extinction, – you'll not die, it cannot be!

XIV

'As for Venice and her people, merely born to bloom and drop,
Here on earth they bore their fruitage, mirth and folly were the
    crop:
What of soul was left, I wonder, when the kissing had to stop?

XV

'Dust and ashes!' So you creak it, and I want the heart to
    scold.
Dear dead women, with such hair too – what's become of all
    the gold
Used to hang and brush their bosoms? I feel chilly and grown
    old.

A
Christmas
Cracker

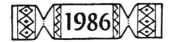

I would rather eat a meal without meat
Than live in a place with no bamboos.
Without meat one may become thin;
Without bamboos one becomes vulgar.

Su Dong-Po
Eleventh century

A self-explanatory letter from the late – and sadly missed – Penelope Betje-
man:

No Telephone Thank God   New House
      [Printed]   Cusop
                                                  Hay-on-Wye
                                                  Hereford

14.i.75

Dear Miss Wilson,

I am very flattered at being asked to appear on the Michael
Parkinson programme but I am no good at TV stuff AT ALL:
1) I have a suet-pudding face   2) I have just knocked all the
crowns off my front teeth   3) I can NEVER think of answers to
questions on the spur of the moment and cannot now even think
of them in the traditional BATH because I have not got one up
here: only a plastic bowl which offers no inspiration.   4) I have
not done anything for some time to bring me into the PUBLIC EYE
so nobody would want to see or hear me   5) I hate coming up to
London in the winter as I like the STORMS down here and am tied
to ponies and dogs   6) IF I ever overcome my perpetual pro-
crastination and write another book I am sure John Gammons
would be very grateful to you for including me in your programme
as I just HAVE to make an effort about publicity at such times.
VERY SORRY . . .

                                         Yours sincerely,
                                         Penelope Betjeman.

'Ours is a Christian army,' thus he said,
'A regiment of bango-men who led.
And ours a Christian navy,' added he,
'Who sailed a thunder-junk upon the sea.'
They better know, than men unwarlike do,
What is an army, and a navy too:
Pray God there may be added, by and by,
Knowledge of what a Christian is, and why;
For somewhat lamely the conception runs
Of a brass-buttoned Jesus, firing guns.

Ambrose Bierce

I have not yet managed to track this poem down, the London Library having surprisingly little of Bierce. What, I wonder, are bango-men?

[Dr Kenneth Sinclair-Loutit writes to me from Rabat, ingeniously suggesting that 'bango-men' may be a corruption of 'Bungo-men', i.e. troops of the Japanese Daimyo, Otomo Yoshishige, who was known as the King of Bungo to the Portuguese. His domain was the north-east corner of Kyushu Island, which is separated from Shikoku by a channel still called the Straits of Bungo. Yoshishige was converted to Christianity by St Francis Xavier in 1578. The Portuguese showed him how to make gunpowder and gave him a musket to copy; within a short time he had made 30,000 of them.

The suggestion may sound a little far-fetched; but nobody has yet come up with a better one.]

A marvellous beginning to a book is that of Bertrand Russell's Autobiography:

> Three passions, simple but overwhelmingly strong, have governed my life: the longing for love, the search for knowledge, and unbearable pity for the suffering of mankind.*

As for book endings, despite the several splendid ones quoted in earlier Crackers; the palm must surely go to Izaak Walton's Life of John Donne:

> He was earnest and unwearied in the search for knowledge: with which his vigorous soul is now satisfied, and employed in a continual praise of that God, that first breathed it into his active body; that body, which once was a Temple of the Holy Ghost, and is now become a small quantity of Christian dust.
>
> But I shall see it reanimated.

* [Edward Marsh records in his book of reminiscences, *A Number of People*, a remark of Bertrand Russell's 'when in a disquisition on the capacity of mankind for misery he said he had never been so unhappy that he would not have been cheered, in an appreciable measure, by the sudden offer of a chocolate cream'.]

And, talking of palms, I once wrote a book about the Sahara in which I noted:

> Date palms are generally held by those who cultivate them to have a considerable capacity for affection; if one of them dies, its neighbours will mourn for it, drooping and ceasing to bear fruit. A female palm, I was told, will even pine away altogether if its lover is felled.

I have recently found corroboration of this remarkable fact in Ammianus Marcellinus. Writing in the 4th century AD about the campaigns of the Emperor Julian the Apostate in Mesopotamia (Book XXIV, Chapter 3), he notes:

> Palm-trees grow there over a great extent of the country, reaching as far as Mesene and the ocean, forming extensive groves. And wherever one goes one sees continually stocks and suckers of palms, from the fruit of which an abundance of honey and wine is made, and the palms themselves are said to be divided into male and female. The two sexes, moreover, can be easily distinguished.
>
> It is also said that the female trees produce fruit when impregnated by the seeds of the male trees, and even that they feel delight in their mutual love: and that this is clearly shown by the fact that they lean towards one another, and cannot be bent back even by strong winds. And if by any unusual accident a female tree is not impregnated by the male seed, it produces nothing but imperfect fruit; and if they cannot find out with what male tree any female tree is in love, they smear the trunk of some tree with the oil which proceeds from her, and then some other tree naturally conceives a fondness for the odour; and these proofs create some belief in the story of their copulation.

When my father was given a peerage in 1952 he found himself looking for a motto for the family crest. That which he eventually chose, Odi et Amo, comes from one of his favourite poets, Catullus. What a memorable couplet it is that those words introduce:

Odi et amo; quare id faciam, fortasse requiris.
    Nescio, sed fieri sentio et excrucior.

I hate and love; you ask, perhaps, how that can be.
    I do not know, yet I feel it happen; and I am in anguish.

A dictionary definition from the Nouveau Petit Larousse Illustré:

Isabelle; (i-za-be-le) *adj.* du nom de l'archiduchesse d'Autriche *Isabelle*, fille de Philippe II, dont le mari assiégeait Ostende et qui fit voeu, dit-on, de ne pas changer de chemise avant la prise de la ville. Celle-ci eut lieu après plus de trois ans, et le nom de la princesse serait resté à la couleur que sa chemise avait prise dans cet intervalle. (On a rapporté quelquefois, mais à tort, cette anecdote à Isabelle la Catholique.) D'une couleur café au lait. *Cheval isabelle*, de couleur isabelle avec les crins et les extrémités noirs.

And another, from the Oxford English Dictionary, *brought to my attention by my friend Robert Bernard Martin:*

Sooterkin: An imaginary kind of afterbirth formerly attributed to Dutch women.

1658. CLEVELAND, *Char. Diurn. Maker* (1677) 103: There goes a Report of the Holland Women, that together with their Children, they are delivered of a Sooterkin, not unlike to a Rat, which some imagine to be the Off-spring of the Stoves . . .

1862. DRAPER, *Intell. Devel. Europe xviii*, (1865) 412: The housewives of Holland no longer bring forth sooterkins by sitting over the lighted chauffers.

I wish it had been 'chauffeurs' . . .

– Is it inconsistent in a Christian professor occasionally to attend a concert?

– As a general rule we should recommend every Christian professor severely to scrutinize his motives and weigh the probable influence of his conduct before embarking on a practice, at the best but questionable.

Youth's Magazine, 1848

When Charles Johnston died earlier this year, many of us mourned a dear friend and the country lost a fine poet. His translations of Pushkin (Eugene Onegin) and Lermontov (The Demon) are the best ever made into English; indeed, it is hard to see how they could possibly be bettered. Extracts may appear in future Crackers; meanwhile, here is an original poem of his:

THE HATCHERY

The shallow conduit shakes in all
Its breadth, and feels the waterfall,
And lets the before-breakfast sun
Light up the trout and, one by one,
Project their shadows, damp and cold,
Across a ground of leaves and mould.
Smoky and plump are those that take
The beams, and solid and opaque.
Others that swim against the light
Would tempt a fainter appetite,
The flimsiest eating, frail as air
And lucid as their watery lair.
Succulent trout, that bask and gleam
And ride immobile, head to stream:
Edible shapes, sun-grilled but cool,
Caught in the aspic of the pool.

And, while remembering Charles, how can one not also remember his inspired couplet on Air Travel in Arabia?

Then Petra flashed by in a wink.
It looked like Eaton Square – *but pink*.

My goddaughter Allegra Huston, who has already contributed more than one item to the Crackers, has now come up with another. She found it in Notes from a Diary, *by Sir Mountstuart E. Grant Duff, GCSI (London, 1897):*

November 10, 1853:

Mr [Thomas Love] Peacock talked to me today at much length about Jeremy Bentham, with whom he had been extremely intimate – dining with him *tête à tête* once a week for years together. He mentioned, amongst other things, that when experiments were being made with Mr Bentham's body after his death, Mr James Mill had one day come into his (Mr Peacock's) room at the India House and told him that there had exuded from Mr Bentham's head a kind of oil, which was almost unfreezable, and which he conceived might be used for the oiling of chronometers which were going into high latitudes. 'The less you say about that, Mill,' said Peacock, 'the better it will be for *you*; because if the fact becomes known, just as we see now in the newspaper advertisements to the effect that a fine bear is to be killed for his grease, we shall be having advertisements to the effect that a fine philosopher is to be killed for his oil.'

Last year's Cracker included Sir Walter Ralegh's lovely poem 'As you came from the holy land Of Walsingham . . .' Here is another poem, this time about the destruction of the shrine by Henry VIII, who had the miraculous image of Our Lady of Walsingham taken to London and burnt at Thomas Cromwell's house in Chelsea, so that 'the people should use no more idolatrye unto it'. It is thought to be by Philip Howard, Earl of Arundel.

In the wrackes of Walsingham
　　Whom should I chuse
But the Queen of Walsingham
　　To be guide to my muse?

Then thou Prince of Walsingham
　　Grant me to frame
Bitter plaintes to rewe thy wrong
　　Bitter woe for thy name.

Bitter was it oh to see
　　The silly sheepe
Murdered by the ravening wolves
　　While the sheephards did sleep.

Bitter was it oh to viewe
　　The sacred vyne
While the gardiners plaied all close
　　Rooted up by the swine.

Bitter bitter oh to behould
　　The grasse to growe
Where the walls of Walsingham
　　So stately did shewe.

Such were the works of Walsingham
　　Where she did stand
Such are the wrackes as nowe do shewe
　　Of that holy land.

Levell levell with the ground
　　The towres doe lye
Which with their golden, glittering tops
　　Pearsed once to the sky.

Where weare gates no gates are nowe,
　　The waies unknowen,
Where the press of peares did pass
　　While her fame was far blowen.

Oules do scrike where the sweetest himnes
    Lately were songe,
Toades and serpents hold their dennes
    Where the palmers did throng.

Weepe weepe O Walsingham,
    Whose dayes are nightes,
Blessings turned to blasphemies,
    Holy deeds to despites.

Sinne is where Our Ladie sate,
    Heaven turned is to Hell,
Sathan sittes where our Lord did swaye,
    Walsingham oh farewell.

Twelve years ago, in the 1974 Cracker, I included a description of the entry of the Emperor Otto III into Charlemagne's tomb. Here is an account – taken from the Annual Register, *2 May 1774 – of a somewhat similar visit: to that of King Edward I of England:*

Some gentlemen of the Society of Antiquaries, being desirous to see how far the actual state of Edward I's body answered to the methods to preserve it, obtained leave to open the large stone sarcophagus, in which it was deposited, on the north side of Edward the Confessor's Chapel. This was accordingly done this morning, when, in a coffin of yellow stone, they found the royal body, in perfect preservation, wrapt in two wrappers, one of them of gold tissue, strongly waxed, and fresh; the outermost more decayed. The corpse was habited in a rich mantle of purple, paned with white, and adorned with ornaments of gilt metal, studded with red and blue stones and pearls. Two similar ornaments lay on his hands. The mantle was fastened on the right shoulder by a magnificent fibula of the same metal, with the same stones and pearls. His face had over it a silken covering, so fine, and so closely fitted to it, as to preserve the features entire. Round his temples was a gilt coronet of *fleurs de lys*. In his hands, which were also entire, were two sceptres of gilt metal; that in the right surmounted by a *Cross Fleuri*, that in the left by three clusters of oak leaves, and a dove on a globe; this sceptre was about five feet long. The feet were enveloped in the mantle and other coverings, but sound, and the toes distinct. The whole length of the corpse was six feet two inches . . . Edward I died at Burgh upon Sands in Cumberland, on his way to Scotland, July 7 1307, in the 68th year of his age.

The Register *does not, however, mention a somewhat awkward little incident which occurred on this occasion. It is reported in* The Olio, '*a posthumous collection (1796) of miscellaneous antiquities, etc.', by Francis Grose:*

Whilst the tomb was open, the Dean of Exeter observed Mr G. to take something privately out of it, and convey it hastily into his waistcoat pocket; this he immediately taxed him with, and insisted that what he had taken should be restored, and replaced in the tomb. Mr G. at first denied it; but Sir Joseph Ayloffe confirming the accusation, a search was insisted on, and the pocket turned inside out, when it was discovered that Mr G. had secreted – not a gold crucifix, nor valuable ring, but a joint of the King's middle finger, which was again deposited in the coffin, to the great displeasure of Mr G. The story was, however, for a while kept secret, but at length was whispered about, and soon became public.

For all compilers of commonplace books, epitaphs are the most perilous of pitfalls. In a way they are too easy: if given half a chance, they tend to overload the whole collection. But they provide too rich a vein of poetry, humour and fantasy to be omitted altogether, especially ones like this:

Here lies the body of Lady O'Looney, great-niece of Burke, commonly called the sublime. She was bland, passionate, and deeply religious; also, she painted in water-colours and sent several pictures to the exhibition. She was first cousin to Lady Jones; and of such is the Kingdom of Heaven.

But the more laconic in style also have their charm. Like that in the curious little Georgian Gothic church of Tetbury in Gloucestershire which reads:

In a vault underneath
lie several of the Saunderses,
late of this parish: particulars
the Last Day will disclose.

In a footnote to the last chapter of Modern Painters, *John Ruskin quotes this extract from a letter written by the father of Charles Kingsley:*

I had taken my mother and a cousin to see Turner's pictures; and, as my mother knows nothing about art, I was taking her down the gallery to look at the large Richmond Park, but as we were passing the Sea-storm, she stopped before it, and I could hardly get her to look at any other picture; and she told me a great deal more about it than I had any notion of, though I have seen many sea-storms. She had been in such a scene on the coast of Holland during the war. When, some time afterwards, I thanked Turner for his permission for her to see the pictures, I told him that he would not guess which had caught my mother's fancy, and then named the picture; and then he said, 'I did not paint it to be understood, but I wished to show what such a scene was like: I got the sailors to lash me to the mast to observe it; I was lashed for four hours and I did not expect to escape, but I felt bound to record it if I did. But no one had any business to like the picture.' 'But,' said I, 'my mother once went through just such a scene, and it brought it all back to her.' 'Is your mother a painter?' 'No.' 'Then she ought to have been thinking of something else.'

When I am gonne, dreeme mee some happinesse,
Nor let thy looks our long-hid love confesse,
Nor praise, nor dispraise mee, nor bless, nor curse
Openly Love's force, nor in bed fright thy Nurse
With midnight startings, crying out, 'Oh, Oh,
Nurse, oh my love is slaine, I saw him goe
O'er the white Alpes alone . . .'

John Donne

Early in 1975, when I was editing a one-volume History of World Architecture, *I decided to commission a 600-word introduction from the renowned engineer, architect and visionary Buckminster Fuller. There arrived, almost by return of post, a 3,500-word article which built up to the following climactic conclusion:*

> We will see the (1) down-at-the-mouth-ends curvature of land civilisation's retrogression from the (2) straight raft line foundation of the Mayans' building foundation lines historically transformed to the (3) smiling, up-end curvature of maritime technology transformed through the climbing angle of wingfoil aeronautics precessing humanity into the verticality of outward-bound rocketry and inward-bound microcosmy, ergo (4) the ultimately invisible and vertically-lined architecture as humans master local environment with invisible electro-magnetic fields while travelling by radio as immortal pattern-integrities.

On reflection, I asked Dr Nikolaus Pevsner instead.

Je suis le ténébreux, le veuf, l'inconsolé,
Le Prince d'Aquitaine à la tour abolie;
Ma seule étoile est morte, et mon luth constellé
Porte le soleil noir de la mélancholie.

Gérard de Nerval

Her Majesty's speech delivered upon the reassembling of Parliament was, as usual, insipid and uninstructive. Its preferred topic was her Majesty's approaching marriage, a matter of little importance or interest to the country, except as it may thereby be burdened with additional and unnecessary expense.

The Times, 18 January 1840.

I have always regretted that the French, having gone to the trouble of inventing new names for the months of the year as part of the Clean Sweep of the Revolution, did not stick to them. They were originally thought up by Fabre d'Eglantine (no bad name in itself), a friend of Danton who admittedly once wrote a rather uninspired poem entitled 'Etude de la Nature' but who was otherwise best known for the song 'Il pleut, il pleut, bergère' and a comedy, Le Philinte de Molière, ou La Suite du Misanthrope, *which had quite a success in 1790. But the months were far and away the best thing he ever did. Most people, I find, can remember some of them; but few – on this side of the Channel at any rate – can recite the whole lot off pat. Here they are:*

Vendémiaire	22 September–21 October
Brumaire	22 October–20 November
Frimaire	21 November–20 December
Nivôse	21 December–19 January
Pluviôse	20 January–19 February
Ventôse	20 February–20 March
Germinal	21 March–19 April
Floréal	20 April–19 May
Prairial	20 May–18 June
Messidor	19 June–19 July
Thermidor	20 July–18 August
Fructidor	19 August–17 September

The dates are accurate only to within a day or two, and there are still five days left unaccounted for; sans-culottides, Fabre called them. But calendars are like that, and for all the scientific earthiness of the Revolution this one seems to have been less accurate than most. Still, they might have kept the names, if nothing else.

I have long enjoyed an intermittent correspondence with a gentleman I have never met – Mr H. C. Bulli, 'Advocate, Supreme Court of India, Ex-Public Prosecutor, UP'. It began when I wrote asking him for copies of his poetry, which I much admired; then one day he sent me his plan for a new banking system for use by his less educated compatriots. I complimented him on it, as a matter of courtesy; and was astonished to find a few months later that it had been published as 'The Norwich–Bulli Method', with an enthusiastic introduction by the then Prime Minister of India, Mr Desai. Since then my name has appeared on Mr Bulli's writing paper as his 'Associate', together with my address and telephone number.

In May 1979 Mr Bulli sent me the following lament – well up to his usual standards – on the execution of Mr Zulfikar Ali Bhutto, former Prime Minister of Pakistan. He told me that Mr Bhutto had asked him two years before for details of the Norwich–Bulli Method, and gave it as his opinion that had these reached Mr Bhutto in time he would still have been alive, and in power.

MARTYR BHUTTO

The great man of Pakistan, the Zulfikar Ali Bhutto,
Was killed on Fourth April Nineteen Seventynine, oh!
Ex-Prime Minister of his country, a noble soul,
Was hanged at the gallows with a foul goal.
A fighter for Pakistan, the Leader Moslem's,
Off-spring of Shah Nawaz, Of Kingly kin's.
The Soul of Pak, Bhutto Ali Zulfikar,
No one will say, is left behind afar.
He galloped on to gallows, for mercy never begged,
With noose on his neck, not one cry he pegged.
Zia, whom he favoured as The Commander In Chief,
Got him hanged treacherously, like a common thief.
Judges were juggled, bayonets shown to the puzzled,
Although named 'Son of Truth', in case it was muzzled.
When the country was in delirium after 'Seventy-One' defeat,
Zulfi took up its reigns [*sic*], brought it up on its feet.
Bangladesh was proclaimed, Pakistan was torn asunder,
He freed the great prisoner, didn't commit blunder.
A leader of the Jinnah and Liaqat Ali Khan type,
Public's Apple of Eyes, and did their tears wipe.
The Military leaders had ruined the whole country,
Came on our Zulfi, and did mend it up all he.
They kicked and cried up against 'rigging' of election,
He sought aid of 'Norwich–Bulli' Method by High Commission.
Sparing not even women, Zia crossed the limit,
Imprisoned 'Nasrat' and 'Benazir', finding it fit!
Secretly they hanged him at two o'clock morn,

Likewise buried him: did the Sky warn?
'Mir Mumtaz' and 'Shah Nawaz' are sons of the Martyr,
Bulli! from London they shall dethrone 'Zia-ul-Err'.

One of the special joys of John Aubrey's Brief Lives *is the unexpected light it sheds on popular heroes. Take this anecdote, for example, about Sir Thomas More:*

In his *Utopia* his lawe is that young people are to see each other stark-naked before marriage. Sir William Roper, of Eltham, in Kent, came one morning, pretty early, to my Lord, with a proposall to marry one of his daughters. My Lord's daughters were then both together abed in a truckle-bed in their father's chamber asleep. He carries Sir William into the chamber and takes the Sheete by the corner and suddenly whippes it off. They lay on their Backs, and their smocks up as high as their arme-pitts. This awakened them, and immediately they turned on their bellies. Quoth Roper, I have seen both sides, and so gave a patt on the buttock he made choice of, sayeing, Thou art mine. Here was all the trouble of the wooeing.

[*After this somewhat cursory examination, Sir William chose Margaret. She seems to have borne her father no permanent grudge: by the merest chance, I have just come upon her entry in the* Oxford Companion to English Literature, *which reads:*

According to Stapleton (1535–98) she purchased the head of her dead father nearly a month after it had been exposed on London Bridge and preserved it in spices until her death. It is believed that it was buried with her. Tennyson alludes to this in 'A Dream of Fair Women':

> . . . her, who clasped in her last trance
> Her murdered father's head.]

When Sir Thomas More was canonized in 1935, the Daily Herald *sent out placards to all the news stands in SW3, bearing the words*

CHELSEA MAN MADE SAINT.

That is, or should be, the object held in view in the organisation of military forces; not so much to wage war as to prevent it, a purpose achieved by making war too dangerous and too onerous for an enemy to enter upon with any hope of final success. No other means has ever been discovered, or ever will be, to prevent war in ages antecedent to the millennium. When armed forces achieve that result they answer their purpose, and no matter what they cost, they are infinitely cheap.

The Military Correspondent
of *The Times*, 6 June 1904

I remember my father once arguing that the idea that armaments produced war was as absurd as the idea that umbrellas produced rain.

... So No. 3 Cmdo were very anxious to be chums with Lord Glasgow so they offered to blow up an old tree stump for him and he was very grateful and said don't spoil the plantation of young trees near it because that is the apple of my eye and they said no of course not we can blow a tree down so that it falls on a sixpence and Lord Glasgow said goodness you are clever and he asked them all to luncheon for the great explosion. So Col. Durnford-Slater DSO said to his subaltern, have you put enough explosive in the tree. Yes, sir, 75 lbs. Is that enough? Yes sir I worked it out by mathematics it is exactly right. Well better put a bit more. Very good sir.

And when Col. D. Slater DSO had had his port he sent for the subaltern and said subaltern better put a bit more explosive in that tree. I don't want to disappoint Lord Glasgow. Very good sir.

Then they all went out to see the explosion and Col. D. S. DSO said you will see that tree fall flat at just that angle where it will hurt no young trees and Lord Glasgow said goodness you are clever.

So soon they lit the fuse and waited for the explosion and presently the tree, instead of falling quietly sideways, rose 50 feet into the air taking with it $\frac{1}{2}$ acre of soil and the whole of the young plantation.

And the subaltern said Sir I made a mistake, it should have been $7\frac{1}{2}$ lbs. not 75.

Lord Glasgow was so upset he walked in dead silence back to his castle and when they came to the turn of the drive in sight of his castle what should they find but that every pane of glass in the building was broken.

So Lord Glasgow gave a little cry and ran to hide his emotion in the lavatory and there when he pulled the plug the entire ceiling, loosened by the explosion, fell on his head.

This is quite true.

E.

The final protestation of truth is always a good sign with Waugh – if not actually of veracity, at least as an indication of something gloriously quotable. At some time unknown in 1931 he ended a letter to Lady Mary and Lady Dorothy Lygon with a P.S.:

I bought a book today called *Twice Round the World with the Holy Ghost*. This is perfectly true.

Lines written by Dorothy Parker during the First World War:

Only, for the nights that were,
Soldier, and the dawns that came,
When in sleep you turn to her,
Call her by my name.

It is some years since we have had any palindromes; here now is a tour de force *which contains what will probably be the last of the species ever to appear in these Crackers – because after this there is really no more to be said. The author is my friend Roy Dean, formerly Deputy High Commissioner in Ghana and twice* The Times Crossword Puzzle *national champion. Since – unlike virtually every other Cracker item – it has never before been published, he particularly asks me to include the following short preface:*

WORD-ROW

In his fascinating book *Language on Vacation* (Scribner's, 1965) Dmitri A. Borgmann discusses single-line palindromes and says:

'The question now arises as to whether or not it is possible to construct a poem consisting entirely of palindromes. In English, this seems to be a feat of Herculean proportions.'

Palindromes can certainly be made to scan, even if they usually come out as meaningless drivel; and the problem is compounded if the lines have to rhyme as well. But what if the verses were the ramblings of an elderly drunk, not knowing whether he was coming or going? One could then visualize a scene in a waterfront bar, and the man's incoherent thoughts as his rheumy eyes roam around the room at the range of liquors on display. The result might be something like the poem 'Senile's Reverie i' Reverse Lines', which has been produced over a period of twenty years.

If I have used any previously published lines, I apologize to their authors. It is notoriously difficult to track down the original source of a palindrome.

Roy Dean
Bromley, September 1989

SENILE'S REVERIE I' REVERSE LINES

I

Sleepless evening, nine. Vessel peels,
Sleek cats yell at alley, stack eels.
Rabelais, send a sadness! I, ale-bar,
Rajah sahib at tab. I hash a jar.
Burton, odd nap, I sip and do not rub
But liven as partner entraps an evil tub.

No, it's a bar, ever a bastion.
No ill imbibe, not one. Bib million,
Zillion US pints. If fist nip sun-oil, Liz,
Sit right, or free beer froth-girt is.
Red neb – a nostril – flirts on a bender,
Red net rabbi rose, so rib bartender.

II
Netta Delia sailed at ten,
Niagara, fall afar again.
Re-rack sack, can snack, cask-carer;
A rare Medoc! O Demerara!
Murder noses on red rum,
Mum, it poses optimum.
To predicate, go get a cider pot,
Toll a renegade, bed a general lot
To claret. Alas, it is a lateral cot.
Warren, slip a Pilsner raw,
Ward, regale me, lager draw;
Walter, aback sir, I risk cabaret law.

III
Night, ninth gin,
Nip ale, lap in.
Malt some most lam;
Marc in I cram,
Gorge, niff of fine grog.
Gong! Get at egg-nog.
Too hot to hoot?
Too tall a toot
To order red root.
Tosspot tops sot
To pay a pot,
Totes in a reviver – anise tot.

IV
Retsina, call a canister;
Ruffino pull upon. If fur,
Laminate pet animal.
Laid rock, lime-milk cordial,
Dude potion sees. No, I tope dud
Dubonnet forever, often. No bud,
No Campari. Did I rap 'Macon'?
No net's a fillip. Ill I fasten on
Yale belt. To bag a bottle belay
Yard aside. Repapered is a dray.
Martini redder in it ram;
Madeira ewer. I tire, wearied am.

V

'S midnight, flew. Twelfth gin dims
Smirnoff – it's put up, stiff on rims.
Dray, pull up yard,
Draught nets tenth guard.
Set ale, drawn inward, elates
Set as serener estates.
No garden, I left. Feline dragon,
No gal faster frets a flagon.
Dial simple hero, more help mislaid,
Diaper motto by baby bottom repaid.
Bilge be mildewed, lime be glib;
Bird imitators rot a timid rib.

VI

Barcarolle, clever revel. Cell or a crab?
Bar delay alerts a wastrel; a Yale drab
Tastes sop, wolfs nuts. Tuns flow possets at
Tart, nor fret away a waterfront rat.
Spill a cold image, keg amid local lips,
Spirits assent. I witness Asti rips.
Strap on gate-man's name-tag. No parts
Straddle if I'd roll. Lord, I field darts,
E'en knots erotic. I to rest on knee;
Emotion's sensuousness, No. I to me.
Pacer in mutual autumn, I recap
Pals as reviled, so red-eyed Eros delivers a slap.

A
Christmas
Cracker

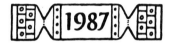

1987

The year 1986 was made memorable for me by my belated discovery of the novels of Professor Robertson Davies, of which I devoured the entire canon, one after the other. Such, indeed, was my delight in them that I felt impelled to write Professor Davies a fan letter – the first, as far as I remember, that I have ever written to an unknown author – and to send him, as a ridiculously inadequate token of my admiration, a set of Crackers. He rewarded me with the following verse of a hymn – from the pen, he assures me, of no less a master than Isaac ('O God our help in ages past') Watts:

> Blest is the man whose bowels move
>   And melt with pity for the poor;
> His soul in sympathising love
>   Feels what his fellow saints endure.
> His heart contrives for their relief
>   More good than his own hands can do:
> He in a time of general grief
>   Finds that his Lord has bowels too.

[In the last days of 1989, when this book was already being prepared for the press, I received a letter from Professor Davies enclosing a fragment he had culled from the Pathetical and Consolatory Poems *of J. Pickering, (Birmingham 1830). It reads as follows:*

> He makes the bitter sweet, the med'cine food,
> And 'all things work together for our good'.
> He knows our frame, and with paternal love
> He chides our follies while His bowels move.]

From Near Home, or, Europe Discovered, *1850:*

Question: What is the religion of the Italians?
Answer: They are Roman Catholics.

Question: What do the Roman Catholics worship?
Answer: Idols and a piece of bread.

Question: Would not God be very angry if He knew that the
          Italians worshipped idols and a piece of bread?
Answer: God *is* very angry.

Sometimes, when night has thickened on the woods,
And we in the house's square security
Read, speak a little, read again,
Read life at second-hand, speak of small things,
Being content and withdrawn for a little hour,
From the dangers and fears that are either wholly absent
Or wholly invading – sometimes a shot rings out,
Sudden and sharp, complete, it has no sequel,
No sequel for us, only the sudden crack
Breaking a silence, followed by a silence.
Too slight a thing for comment, slight and unusual,
A shot in the dark, fired by a hand unseen,
At a life unknown, finding or missing the target,
Bringing death? bringing hurt? teaching perhaps escape?
Escape from a present threat, a threat recurrent,
Or ending once and for all? But we read on,
Since the shot was not at our hearts, since the mark was not
Your heart or mine, not this time, my companion.

Victoria Sackville-West

Macaulay describes the consequences of the War of the Austrian Succession (1741–8):

But the selfish rapacity of the King of Prussia gave the signal to his neighbours. His example quieted their sense of shame. His success led them to underrate the difficulty of dismembering the Austrian monarchy. The whole world sprang to arms. On the head of Frederic is all the blood which was shed in a war which raged during many years and in every quarter of the globe, the blood of the column of Fontenoy, the blood of the mountaineers who were slaughtered at Culloden. The evils produced by his wickedness were felt in lands where the name of Prussia was unknown; and, in order that he might rob a neighbour whom he had promised to defend, black men fought on the coast of Coromandel, and red men scalped each other by the Great Lakes of North America.

*Anne Thackeray Ritchie was the daughter of William Makepeace Thack-
eray and – although she is today largely forgotten – a distinguished novelist
in her own right. Here is her description of her meeting, as a girl of about
eighteen, with George Sand:*

She was a stout middle-aged woman, dressed in a stiff watered-
silk dress, with a huge cameo, such as people then wore, at her
throat. Her black shiny hair shone like polished ebony, she had a
heavy red face, marked brows, great dark eyes; there was something – however shall I say it? – rather fierce, defiant, and set in
her appearance, powerful, sulky; she frightened one a little. 'That
is George Sand,' said Mrs Sartoris, bending her head and making
a friendly sign to the lady with her eye-glasses. The figure also
bent its head, but I don't remember any smile or change of that
fixed expression.

*The only other description I know of George Sand is Sainte-Beuve's, who
– according to George Lyttelton in one of his letters to Rupert Hart-Davis
– said of her that 'she had a great soul and a perfectly enormous bottom'. I
know, however, a good deal more about Lady Ritchie, thanks to the
admirable biography of her by Winifred Gerin and her obituary, by her
step-niece Virginia Woolf, which appeared in the* Times Literary Supple-
ment *of 6 March 1919 and of which the following is an extract:*

We feel that we have been in the same room with the people
she describes. Very likely the great man has said nothing memorable, perhaps he has not even spoken; occasionally her memory is
not of seeing him but of missing him; never mind – there was an
ink-pot, perhaps a chair, he stood in this way, he held his hat just
so, and miraculously and indubitably there he is before our eyes.
Again and again it has happened to us to trace down our
conception of one of the great figures of the past not to the stout
official biography consecrated to him, but to some little hint or
fact or fancy dropped lightly by Lady Ritchie in passing, as a bird
alights on a branch, picks off the fruit, and leaves the husk for another.

*[Peter Levi writes: 'Did you know Mrs Ritchie had the whiskers shaved
from the marble bust of Thackeray in the Abbey?']*

The subject of Virginia Woolf and Lady Ritchie – at this time still Mrs Ritchie, since her husband (who had first proposed to her when he was still at Eton, despite the fact that she was seventeen years older than himself) was knighted only in 1907 – leads me ineluctably on to the story of the election of Sir Leslie Stephen to the presidency of the London Library. On 7 December 1892, Stephen wrote to his friend Charles Eliot Norton:

> . . . By the way, I have received an honour which pleases me and rather amuses me. I have been elected President of the London Library . . . It amused me because the election is made by the Committee, and the first proposal was to elect Gladstone. Somebody then proposed me, and modesty induced me to retire from the room. Otherwise I should have liked to hear a comparison between my claims and those of the great man. As it is, he is my Vice-, or one of them, and I am one of the few people who can be called his superior . . .

His daughter Virginia was only ten years old at the time, so it was still some years before she would marry Leonard Woolf and achieve literary fame of her own. But she was already the self-appointed editor of, and principal contributor to, The Hyde Park Gate News *– the Stephens lived at No. 22 – Vol. ii, No. 45 of which contained the following item:*

Mr Leslie Stephen whose immense literary powers are well known is now the President of the London Library which as Lord Tennyson was before him and Carlyle was before Tennyson is justly esteemed a great honour. Mrs Ritchie the daughter of Thackeray who came to luncheon the next day expressed her delight by jumping from her chair and clapping her hands in a childish manner but none the less sincerely. The greater part of Mrs Stephen's joy lies in the fact that Mr Gladstone is only vice-president. She is not at all of a 'crowy' nature but we can forgive any woman for triumphing when her husband gets above Mr Gladstone. We think that the London Library has made a very good choice in putting Mr Stephen before Mr Gladstone as although Mr Gladstone may be a first-rate politician he cannot beat Mr Stephen in writing. But as Mr Stephen with that delicacy and modesty which with many other good qualities is always eminent in the great man's manner went out of the room when the final debate was taking place we cannot oblige our readers with more of the interesting details.

It was indeed difficult to get above Mr Gladstone. When he sat his final examinations at Christ Church in 1831, he began his paper on Moral Philosophy thus:

It will be my endeavour, in the consideration of this question, to adhere as closely as possible, in point of division and arrangement, to the order suggested by the form in which it has been proposed. The principal heads may thus be briefly stated:

I.   To discuss $\left\{\begin{array}{l}\text{1. the absolute}\\ \text{2. the relative}\end{array}\right\}$ compatibility of virtue and self-denial.

II. To contrast the conclusion thus obtained with the Stoical doctrine of ἀπάθεια.
     Also with a particular reference to Aristotle.

III. By considering the nature and office of conscience, to inquire how far the question whether it is factitious or innate is affected by anything hitherto stated.

According to Jan Morris's The Oxford Book of Oxford, *his paper was fourteen pages long, and ended:*

As much has been done as time and hesitation would allow me. There is not even time to reperuse.

And the same splendid volume tells us that when at his viva voce the examiners, having cross-examined him thoroughly on one subject, then announced their intention of passing on to the next, he indignantly expostulated: 'No, if you please, Sir, we will not leave it yet!' He got, it need hardly be said, a Double First.

Frankly, I prefer the performance of one Peter Ralli, who was at New College in the early 1920s. Sir Maurice Bowra wrote in his memoirs of how

... when he took History Finals in 1922, he answered very few questions, and then briefly, one example being the single sentence, written in a huge, flowing hand:
'Her subjects wanted Queen Elizabeth to abolish tunnage and poundage, but the splendid creature stood firm.'

There was a fine sentence, too, in an essay on the suffragette movement submitted for the 1984 Batsford Townsend-Warner History Prize for Preparatory Schools:

The ladies had to have the vote, or the country would have been swarming with hordes of frenzied parlour-maids.

The last words of General John Sedgwick, killed in May 1864 at the Battle of Spotsylvania:

Why, they couldn't hit an elephant at this dist . . .

The 1978 *Cracker* contained a beautiful sonnet to Sleep, by Samuel Daniel. Here is what must, I think, be its nearest French equivalent. It is by Pontus de Tyard. Few people remember him now, but he was a major figure in his time: as well as a poet, he was a bishop (of Chalon-sur-Saône), a philosopher, a stalwart monarchist, a bibliophile and a considerable connoisseur of wine. He was born in 1511, and died – having become a close friend of Henri IV – in 1605, at the age of ninety-four.

Père du doux repos, Sommeil, père du Songe,
    Maintenant que la nuit, d'une grande ombre obscure,
    Fait à cet air sérein humide couverture,
Viens, Sommeil désiré, et dans mes yeux te plonge.
Ton absence, Sommeil, languissamment allonge
    Et me fait plus sentir la peine que j'endure.
    Viens, Sommeil, l'assoupir et la rendre moins dure,
Viens abuser mon mal de quelque doux mensonge.
Jà le muet silence un escadron conduit
    De fantômes ballant dessous l'aveugle nuit;
    Tu me dédaignes seul qui te suis tant dévot.
Viens, Sommeil désiré, m'environner la tête,
    Car, d'un voeu non menteur, un bouquet je t'apprête
    De ta chère morelle et de ton cher pavot.

Death is nothing at all ... I have only slipped away into the next room ... I am I and you are you ... whatever we were to each other, that we are still. Call me by my old familiar name, speak to me in the easy way which you always used. Put no difference into your tone; wear no forced air of solemnity or sorrow. Laugh as we always laughed at the little jokes we enjoyed together. Play, smile, think of me, pray for me. Let my name be ever the household word that it always was. Let it be spoken without effect, without the ghost of a shadow on it. Life means all that it ever meant. It is the same as it ever was; there is absolutely unbroken continuity. What is this death but a negligible accident? Why should I be out of mind because I am out of sight? I am but waiting for you, for an interval, somewhere very near just around the corner ... All is well.

Henry Scott Holland

Derek Parker, in the spring 1992 edition of The Author, *points out that this must be a conscious or unconscious echo of a sermon preached by John Donne on Easter Day 1627 in St Paul's:*

Thus much we may learn from these Heathens, that if the dead, and we, be not upon one floore, nor under one story, yet we are under one roofe. We think not a friend lost, because he is gone into another roome, nor because he has gone into another Land; And into another world, no man is gone; for that Heaven, which God created, and this world, is all one world ...

Madame de Staël said much the same thing:

La mort ne nous sépare pas; elle ne fait que nous rendre invisible.

Last year's Cracker began with a quatrain by the eleventh-century Chinese poet Su Dong-Po. Here is another brief work by the same master, contributed by my friend Rosemary Scott, of the Percival David Foundation for Chinese Art. The translation is by Arthur Waley.

Families, when a child is born,
Want it to be intelligent.
I, through intelligence,
Having wrecked my whole life,
Only hope the baby will prove
Ignorant and stupid.
Then he will crown a tranquil life
By becoming a Cabinet Minister.

Pliny in his natural history reporteth of *Hedg-hogs*, that having been abroad to *provide* their store, and returning home *laden* with nuts and fruit, if the least *Filbert* fall but off, they will in a pettish humour, *fling* down all the rest, and *beat* the ground for very anger with their bristles.

William Barlow
Spencer's Things New and Old, 1658

In the 1982 Cracker I quoted a few favourite extracts from Paradise Lost. *Inevitably, however, in a work of such length, there are occasional moments when the poet seems to be on somewhat less than tip-top form. I am not sure, for example, that those lines from Book IV are entirely happy where Adam, in conversation with his wife, refers to*

> Our walks at noon, with branches overgrown,
> That mock our scant manuring.

But my vote for the worst bit of all would unquestionably go to the following, also from Book IV:

> This evening from the Sun's decline arriv'd
> Who tells of som infernal Spirit seen
> Hitherward bent (who could have thought?) escap'd
> The barrs of Hell, on errand bad no doubt.

The same Book also contains a description of our first parents retiring for the night – in which, however, it regrettably omits to mention whether or not they brushed their teeth. The Weekend Review *accordingly announced, in September 1931, a competition to make good this omission. As was perhaps to be expected, the first prize was won by Sir Edward Marsh:*

> [. . . and eas'd the putting off
> These troublesome disguises which wee wear,]
> Yet pretermitted not the strait Command,
> Eternal, indispensable, to off-cleanse
> From their white elephantin Teeth the stains
> Left by those tastie Pulps that late they chewd
> At supper. First from a salubrious Fount
> Our general Mother, stooping, the pure Lymph
> Insorb'd, which, mingl'd with tart juices prest
> From pungent Herbs, on sprigs of Myrtle smeard,
> (Then were not Brushes) scrub'd gumms more impearl'd
> Than when young *Telephus* with *Lydia* strove
> In mutual bite of Shoulder and ruddy Lip.
> This done (by Adam too no less) the pair
> [Straight side by side were laid . . .]

The mordacious Telephus and Lydia will be found in Horace, Odes, *I, xiii. Meanwhile here is one more quotation from Book IV, taken from the lovely description of the naked Eve:*

> She, as a veil down to the slender waist,
> Her unadorned golden tresses wore
> Dishevelled, but in wanton ringlets waved
> As the vine curls her tendrils.

How well, I wonder, was Paradise Lost *known to the Rev. Charles Lutwidge Dodgson, alias Lewis Carroll? And what prompts this seemingly irrelevant question? The next page will tell.*

In 1974, Sotheby's auctioned a set of galley proofs containing a previously unknown passage which had been written by Lewis Carroll as part of Chapter VIII of Through the Looking Glass, *but which he had subsequently decided to omit. It was published separately in 1977, and includes a typical nonsense poem, the first two verses of which seem to me as good as anything Carroll ever did in the genre. Here is an extract:*

[The Wasp] untied the handkerchief as he spoke, and Alice looked at his wig in great surprise. It was bright yellow like the handkerchief, and all tangled and tumbled about like a heap of seaweed. 'You could make your wig very much neater,' she said, 'if only you had a comb.'

'What, you're a bee, are you?' the Wasp said, looking at her with more interest. 'And you've got a comb. Much honey?'

'It isn't that kind,' Alice hastily explained. 'It's to comb hair with, – your wig's so very rough, you know.'

'I'll tell you how I came to wear it,' the Wasp said. 'When I was young, you know, my ringlets used to wave –'

A curious idea came into Alice's head. Almost every one she had met had repeated poetry to her, and she thought she would try if the Wasp couldn't do it too. 'Would you mind saying it in rhyme?' she asked very politely.

'It ain't what I'm used to,' said the Wasp: 'however I'll try; wait a bit.' He was silent for a few moments, and then began again –

> 'When I was young, my ringlets waved
>   And curled and crinkled round my head;
> And then they said "You should be shaved,
>   And wear a yellow wig instead."
>
> 'But when I followed their advice,
>   And they had studied the effect,
> They said I did not look so nice
>   As they had ventured to expect.
>
> 'They said it did not fit, and so
>   It made me look extremely plain;
> But what was I to do, you know?
>   My ringlets would not grow again . . .'

He pointed out, too, how difficult it would be to break off the engagement at the eleventh hour.

'But that's just the beauty of the eleventh hour. That's what it's there for, surely,' she said.

Maurice Baring
Cat's Cradle

A slightly abridged (but otherwise unchanged) article by Kenneth Langbell, which appeared in the Bangkok Post *on Saturday 27 May, 1967:*

The recital last evening in the Chamber Music Room of the Erawan Hotel by US pianist Myron Kropp can only be described by this reviewer as one of the most interesting experiences in a very long time. Mr Kropp had chosen the title 'An Evening with Bach'; the evening opened with the Toccata and Fugue in D minor. As I have mentioned on several other occasions, the Baldwin concert grand needs constant attention: in this humidity the felts tend to swell, causing the occasional key to stick, which apparently was the case last evening with the D in the second octave.

Some who attended the performance later questioned whether the awkward key justified some of the language which was heard coming from the stage during softer passages of the fugue. However, one member of the audience, who had sent his children out of the room by the midway point, commented that the workman who greased the stool might have done better to use some of the grease on the second octave D key. Indeed, Mr Kropp's stool had more than enough grease, and during one passage in which the music was particularly violent he was turned completely around. Whereas before his remarks had been largely aimed at the piano and were therefore somewhat muted, to his surprise and that of those in the Chamber Music Room he found himself addressing himself directly to the audience.

By the time the audience had regained its composure Mr Kropp appeared to be somewhat shaken. Nevertheless he swivelled himself back into position and, leaving the D major fugue unfinished, commenced on the Fantasia and Fugue in G minor. Why the G key in the third octave chose that particular time to begin sticking I hesitate to guess. However Mr Kropp himself did nothing to help matters when he began using his feet to kick the lower portion of the piano instead of operate the pedals. Possibly it was this jarring, or the un-Bach-like hammering to which the sticking keyboard was being subjected: something caused the right front leg of the piano to buckle slightly forward, leaving the entire instrument listing at approximately a 35-degree angle. A gasp went up from the audience, for if the piano had actually fallen several of Mr Kropp's toes, if not both his feet, would surely have been broken.

It was with a sigh of relief, therefore, that the audience saw Mr Kropp slowly rise from his stool and leave the stage. A few men in the back of the room began clapping, and when Mr Kropp reappeared a moment later it seemed he was responding to the ovation. Apparently, however, he had left to get the red-handled fire axe which was hung backstage in case of fire, for when he returned that was what he had in his hand.

My first reaction at seeing Mr Kropp begin to chop at the left leg of the grand piano was that he was attempting to make it tilt at the same angle as the right leg. However, when the weakened legs finally collapsed altogether with a great crash and Mr Kropp continued to chop, it became obvious to all that he had no intention of going on with the concert.

The ushers, who had heard the snapping of piano wires and splintering of sounding board from the dining room, came rushing in and, with the help of the hotel manager, two Indian watchmen and a passing police corporal, finally succeeded in disarming Mr Kropp and dragging him off the stage.

The newspapers in the past few months have been full of alarming articles about the industrial pollution of the Rhine – which is no longer, clearly, any place for maidens. But the situation is not recent: it was already pretty bad in Wagner's day, and even in that of Samuel Taylor Coleridge, who complained thus about it after a visit in 1799 – giving incidentally, a completely new dimension to the concept of Eau de Cologne:

In Köln, a town of monks and bones,
And pavements fanged with murderous stones,
And rags, and hags, and hideous wenches,
I counted two and seventy stenches,
All well defined, and several stinks!
Ye Nymphs that reign o'er sewers and sinks,
The river Rhine, it is well known,
Doth wash your city of Cologne;
But tell me, Nymphs! what power divine
Shall henceforth wash the river Rhine?

[*I wonder why Cologne left such a lasting impression on Coleridge; twenty-nine years later it literally drove him to drink. In 1828 he wrote:*

ON MY JOYFUL DEPARTURE
from the same city

As I am a rhymer,
And now at least a merry one,
Mr Mum's Rudesheimer
And the church of St Geryon
Are the two things alone
That deserve to be known
In the body-and-soul-stinking town of Cologne.]

Here lies Dame Mary Page
Relict of Sir Gregory Page, Bart.
She departed this life, March 4th, 1728,
In the 56th year of her age.
In 67 months she was tapped 66 times, and
Had taken away 240 gallons of water,
without ever repining at her case,
Or ever fearing the operation.

I first heard the following verses in my nursery, recited on an old HMV record by Stanley Holloway. They are by Marriott Edgar – who was, I believe, the half-brother of Edgar Wallace. For best results they should be read aloud, in a heavy Yorkshire accent.

I'll tell of the Battle of 'Astings,
As 'appened in days long gone by,
When Duke William became King of England
And 'Arold got shot in the eye.

It were this way – one day in October
The Duke, who were always a toff,
'Avin' no battles on at the moment,
'Ad given the lads a day off.

They'd all taken boats to go fishin',
When some chap said in Conqueror's ear,
'Let's go and put breeze up the Saxons,'
Said William, ''Ere, that's an idea.'

Then, turnin' around to his soldiers,
'E lifted 'is big Norman voice,
Shoutin' ''Ands up who's comin' to England,'
(That were swank, as they 'adn't no choice.)

They started away about tea-time,
The sea was so calm and so still,
And at a quarter to ten the next mornin'
They arrived at a place called Bex'ill.

King 'Arold came up as they landed,
'Is face full of venom and 'ate;
'E said, 'If you've come for t'regatta,
You've got 'ere just six weeks too late.'

At that William rose, cool but 'aughty,
And said, 'give us none of your cheek.
You'd best 'ave your throne reupholstered,
I'll be wantin' to use it next week.'

When 'Arold 'eard this 'ere defiance,
With rage 'e turned purple and blue,
And shouted some rude words in Saxon,
To which William answered, 'And you!'

'Twere a beautiful day for a battle.
The Normans set off with a will,
And when both sides was duly assembled
They tossed for the top of the 'ill.

King 'Arold, 'e won the advantage,
On the 'ill-top 'e took up 'is stand,
With 'is knaves and 'is cads all round 'im,
On 'is horse, with 'is 'awk in 'is 'and.

The Normans 'ad nowt in their favour,
Their chance of a vict'ry seemed small,
For the slope of the field were against 'em,
And the wind in their faces an' all.

The kick-off were sharp at two-thirty;
As soon as the whistle 'ad went,
Both sides started bangin' each other,
Till the swine-'erds could 'ear 'em in Kent.

The Saxons 'ad best line of forwards,
Well armed, both with buckler and sword,
But the Normans 'ad best combination,
And when 'alf-time came neither 'ad scored.

So the Duke called 'is cohorts together,
And said, 'Let's pretend that we're beat;
Once we get Saxons down on the level
We'll cut off their means of retreat.'

So they ran, and the Saxons ran after,
Just exactly as William 'ad planned,
Leavin' 'Arold alone on the 'ill-top,
On 'is 'orse, with 'is 'awk in 'is 'and.

When Conqueror saw what 'ad 'appened,
A bow and an arrer 'e drew,
'E went right up to 'Arold an' shot 'im;
'E were off-side – but what could they do?

The Normans turned round in a fury,
And gave back both parry and thrust,
Till the fight were all over bar shoutin'
And you couldn't see Saxons for dust.

And after the battle were over,
They found 'Arold so stately and grand,
Sittin' there with an eye full of arrer,
On 'is 'orse, with 'is 'awk in 'is 'and.

I have always considered complaints of ill usage contemptible, whether from a seduced disappointed girl or a turned-out Prime Minister.

Lord Melbourne

Vergebens werden ungebundne Geister
Nach der Vollendung reiner Höhe streben.
Wer Grosses will, muss sich zusammenraffen;
In der Beschränkung zeigt sich erst der Meister,
Und das Gesetz nur kann uns Freiheit geben.

These lines of Goethe can be translated

In vain will unrestricted spirits strive
To reach the clear serene of their fulfilment.
He who seeks greatness must confine himself;
For mastery is seen in limitation
And only law can give us liberty.

Compare Wordsworth's sonnet 'Nuns fret not at a convent's narrow room', where he speaks of 'the weight of too much liberty'. Pope also makes much the same point:

Thus *Rules* of old discovered, not devised,
Are Nature still, but Nature methodized;
Nature, like liberty, is but restrained
By the same laws which first herself ordained.

They wander in deep woods, in mournful light,
Amid long reeds and drowsy-headed poppies,
And lakes where no wave laps, and voiceless streams,
Upon whose banks in the dim light grow old
Flowers that were once bewailed names of kings.

From Helen Waddell's Medieval Latin Lyrics: *a translation of the* Silva Myrtea *of Ausonius.*

Here is Procopius, writing in the sixth century AD about an island off France which he calls Brittia. The ancients, he tells us, built a wall across it – though admittedly he says it runs from north to south – so it is hard to believe that he can be talking of anywhere except Britain. He tells us too – in De Bello Gothico, *iv, 20 – that the fertile and populous eastern part was cut off by the wall from a barren western expanse, crawling with snakes, in which no man could live for an hour. He goes on:*

The coast of the continent over against Brittia is dotted with villages, in which dwell fishermen, husbandmen, merchants, who serve the Kings of the Franks but pay them no tribute, being excused by reason of the service which I am about to describe. They understand that they have it in charge to conduct by turns the souls of the dead to the opposite shore. Those upon whom the service devolves, at nightfall betake themselves to sleep, though waiting their summons. As the night grows old, an unseen hand knocks at their doors, the voice of an unseen person calls them to their toil. Then they spring from their couches and run to the shore. They understand not what necessity constrains them thus to act: they know only that they *are* constrained. At the water's edge they see barks not their own, with no visible passengers on board, yet so deeply loaded that there is not a finger's breadth between the water and the rowlocks. They bend to their oars, and in one hour they reach the island of Brittia, which, in their own barks, they can scarce reach in a night and a day, using both oar and sail. Arrived at the other side, as soon as they understand that the invisible disembarkation has taken place, they return, and now their boats are so lightly laden that only the keel is in the water. They see no form of man sailing with them or leaving the ship, but they hear a voice which seems to call each one of the shadowy passengers by name, to recount the dignities which they once held, and to tell their fathers' names. And if women are of the party, the voice pronounces the names of the husbands with whom they lived on earth. Such are the appearances which are vouched for by the men who dwell in those parts.

And not only by those men, either. Procopius adds that he scarcely likes to repeat the story, so like a fable does it sound; and yet, he says, it is attested by such vast numbers of people who have witnessed this strange phenomenon that he cannot bring himself entirely to reject it.

Heaven were not Heaven were the Gods not there,
And where you are 'tis Heaven everywhere.

Written, in a late seventeenth- or early eighteenth-century hand, in the British Museum copy of Alexander Browne's 'The Art of Painting in Miniature', 1669.

A year or two ago my friend Michael Severne sent me a copy of a letter, probably written some time in the 1950s – there is unfortunately no precise date – by his uncle, Rowland Burden-Muller, who was born in 1891. Apart from a brief introductory paragraph, I reproduce it in full.

My own first memories of Florence were slight, social and Victorian. It was the day of Ouida and of Aunt Etta's friend Vernon Lee, and of mother's friend Janet Ross who lived at Poggio Gherardo, fought with Ouida, and made wonderful vermouth from a special recipe of Lorenzo de' Medici given her by the family as a secret. She also wrote an excellent cookery book – *Leaves from a Tuscan Kitchen* – which you should have. Then there was Mrs Maquay, wife of the local British banker, driving in her victoria in the Cascine with an aura of unction and esteem. My Aunt Agatha's husband, Lord Westbury, was constantly inheriting fortunes from injudicious friends and constantly ran through them. An adjunct to one of these inheritances was a peculiar Castello di Vincigliata at Fiesole, over-faithfully restored in the medieval manner by a Mr Leader and possessing every ancient inconvenience. Lord Westbury seldom went there, preferring to indulge himself in his two passions of shooting and gambling. When the shooting season in Yorkshire was over he left for Monte Carlo where he shot clay pigeon and gambled, once losing a million pounds in one year, thus establishing a record for one individual, so the Compagnie des Bains de Mer presented him with a gold medal which became his most precious possession and he wished to have it buried with him. When quite old he committed suicide, preceded in like manner by his son, an Egyptologist, who had helped Lord Carnarvon and Howard Carter to open Tutenkamen's tomb. His grandson, the present Lord Westbury, lives in Rome where he is working on a history of Roman gastronomy.

In those days I saw more of Venice where Aunt Enid [Lady Layard] lived at the Palazzo Cà Cappello mourning, in widow's weeds *à la* Maria Stuart, a husband who had died some ten years before, after a useful life discovering the Ruins of Nineveh and later as Ambassador to the Porte. However, her mourning did not preclude an active social life, with receptions every evening during the month of April: her own on Thursday evenings, the Brandolins on Friday, with remaining evenings taken by the Noces, della Grazias, Morosinis and others. To these, at 14, I was taken so that I should learn to conduct myself appropriately in polite society. On returning home at 1.30 a.m. I was made to

251

stand beneath Carpaccio's *Visit of the Three Magi*, now in the National Gallery, and recite the names, in full with correct titles and proper precedence, of all the persons to whom I had been introduced that evening. Meanwhile Aunt Enid sipped her barley water before going to bed. The mornings started with most of us assembling in the dining room for breakfast, a meal usually interrupted for me since I had to go into the gallery and draw a faded green silk curtain over Gentile Bellini's portrait of Sultan Mohammed in order to protect it from the depredations of the parrot while taking its morning bath. I could never understand why the parrot's cage had to keep company with the Sultan.

On several mornings each week I was sent with Signor Malagola, Keeper of the Archives, 'to see the sights', occasionally accompanied by the vastly dull Princess Stephanie, widow of Crown Prince Rudolph of Austria, a lady-in-waiting and two dachshunds. My mother, fearful of my growing state, insisted on my wearing my Eton suit so as all possible use should be extracted from its cost and, being very Scotch, she insisted that I should top it with a Scotch bonnet with flowing ribbons. Thus garbed, I was taught to row the gondola, surreptitiously, by Ricardo and Giovanni, Aunt Enid's two charming gondoliers. One might have thought that such a sight upon the Grand Canal would have attracted some attention; but the spirit of the nineteenth century still hovered over the twentieth and individuality was rampant. Also I was a Victorian child, obedient and passive and quite devoid of self-consciousness. I suppose a modern child would have rebelled or had to be sent to a psychiatrist.

In those days the campanile had just collapsed and there were only three motor boats in the city and no hotels on the Lido, which can hardly have changed since Byron rowed there. Aunt Enid owned a rush hut, a forerunner of today's cabanas; and sometimes we went there for a picnic. Gondolas were sent ahead with the chef and a couple of *garçons de cuisine*, and a butler and a pair of footmen who placed in position three easels for Aunt Enid, Princess Stephanie and Susie Duchess of Somerset who enjoyed painting in water-colour, thus creating a scene in the manner of Boudin. Being under 15 years of age I was permitted to bathe, and later we were served a six-course collation in the rush hut by the butler and footmen with cotton gloves, returning to Venice by sunset.

The three motor launches belonged to the Spanish Pretender, who also owned an aged white parrot reputedly over 120 years old, to Val Prinsep, the artist son of Watts's patron from Little Holland House, and to a newly arrived American couple, not yet acknowledged by Venetian society. Often we had tea with old Mr and Mrs Eden in their garden on the Giudecca, the largest in

Venice, and nearby was the small nursing home founded by Aunt Enid for British sailors. Sometimes I went out with Val Prinsep or the immensely fat and delightful Clara Montalba when they went sketching, for painting in water-colour was a fashionable vocation. The Prinsep boys were at Eton with me and, occasionally, I got away to see them, although Aunt Enid disapproved of the family as being 'very bohemian', and Mrs Prinsep's father, Mr Leland, had made a scandal with Mr Whistler over the decoration of his dining room.* On Sundays I sang in the choir of the English church, conducted with her fan by Helen Lady Radnor who took her pet gondolier home to Longford Castle in Wiltshire where he rowed her on the lake as part of his duties. The organ was played by Sir Hubert Miller, and was blown by his pet gondolier who was very handsome. Then there were luncheons with Mrs Browning, Pen's wife, who, as a disciple of Dr Fletcher, chewed her food 40 times before swallowing, a method my mother made me adopt at once. Also we were taken on an inspection of the ancient island lunatic asylum, where Mrs Cavendish Bentinck, arrayed in chiffon and pearls, prodded a female lunatic in the buttocks with her parasol exclaiming, 'Do tell me, what is wrong with that one?' Aunt Enid had a *penchant* for minor royalty, a social pest now fortunately extinct, and they were a cause for much entertaining. I remember a beautiful reception for mother's friend, Princess Charlotte of Saxe Meiningen, given by the Duca della Grazia at the Palazzo Vendramin – the deathplace of Wagner – where there were two footmen in eighteenth-century costume outside every door and an orchestra brought from Vienna for the occasion; but I can also remember the trouble I encountered from my mother because of the difficulty I had in saying easily '*grossherzoglicher Hochheit*' when talking to an archduke. For a boy of 14 it was quite a mouthful. It was a period of personalities, of parties, and of palazzos still inhabited by Venetians. Receptions had replaced the Ridotto but pleasure, if sedate, was in the air. Venice was gaily international, whereas Florence was intellectually international, yet somewhat provincial. Of the Italians, the della Grazias, Brandolins, Noces and Countess Morosini entertained frequently, and Aunt Enid, Lady Radnor, Lady Helen Vincent and Sir Hubert Miller of the English. America was represented by the Ralph Curtises of the Palazzo Barbaro whose father was said to have had to leave Boston after losing his temper and pulling a neighbour's nose on the train. The Countess Morosini and Lady Helen Vincent were famous beauties, one dark and the other fair. The former was

---

* He was actually F. R. Leyland. The famous Peacock Room is now to be seen, reconstructed, in the Freer Art Gallery of Washington D.C. – J.J.N.

greatly admired by the German Emperor who sent her his portrait after visiting Venice in his yacht. Many of these figures were caricatured by 'Baron Corvo' in his book *The Pursuit of the Whole and the Past.** It was the period of the English occupation and before the real American invasion when Venice became a fashionable summer resort. In those days the season closed in May.

These are merely the memories of a 14-year-old schoolboy and therefore unimportant in themselves and belonging to a superficial world – too trivial to be of interest, yet too long for a letter. I am quite ashamed of making you the victim of these silly memories but, when old, one's mind is apt to revert to one's youth at the slightest provocation. Unfortunately my mind is a sieve rather than a warehouse, with the city and its art as a background.

---

* Properly, *The Desire and Pursuit of the Whole.* – J.J.N.

A Christmas Cracker

Sir Thomas More, Lord Chancellour: his Countrey-howse was at Chelsey, in Middlesex, where Sir John Danvers built his howse. Where the gate is now, adorned with two noble Pyramids, then stood anciently a Gate-house, which was flatt at the top, leaded, from whence there is a most pleasant prospect of the Thames and the fields beyond. On this place the Lord Chancellour More was wont to recreate himself and contemplate. It happened one time that a Tom of Bedlam came up to him, and had a Minde to have throwne him from the battlements, saying Leap, Tom, leap. The Chancellour was in his gowne, and besides ancient and not able to struggle with such a strong fellowe. My Lord had a little dog. Sayd he, Let us first throwe the dog downe, and see what sporte that will be. So the dog was throwne over. This is very fine sport, sayd my Lord, Let us fetch him up, and try once more. While the mad man was goeing downe, My Lord fastned the dore, and called for help, but ever after kept the dore shutt.

This year's Prize for Unfortunate Imagery (PFUI) is awarded to Richard Crashaw (1612?–49). A magical poet at his best, he sets off at a spanking pace, then tends quite suddenly to miss his footing and comes, not unrefreshingly, a nasty cropper. I quoted one instance of this in the first-ever Cracker of 1970; it describes the weeping Magdalen following Christ, and runs:

> And now where'er he strays,
> Among the Galilean mountains,
>   Or more unwelcome ways,
> He's followed by two faithful fountains;
> Two walking baths; two weeping motions;
> Portable and compendious oceans . . .

Plumbing metaphors, I suppose, are always dangerous in poetry; Crashaw easily caps the above effort with a passage from his 'Shepherd's Hymn':

> Welcome! though not to gold or silk
> To more than Caesar's birthright is:
> Two sister-seas of virgin-milk,
> With many a rarely-tempered kiss
> That breathes at once both Maid and Mother,
> Warms in the one, cools in the other.

A rum cove, Crashaw: brought up in a strictly puritan family, he became a convert to Rome – a courageous step to take in seventeenth-century England – and ended his life as a junior canon at Loreto, where he died. His personal habits seem to have been unusual too, if we are to believe his friend Thomas Carre:

> What he might eate or weare he took no thought:
> His needfull foode he rather found than sought.
> He seeks no downes, no sheetes, his bed's still made.
> If he can find a chaire or stoole, he's lay'd;
> When day peepes in, he quitts his restless rest,
> And still, poore soule, before he's up he's dres't.

Mr Houghton, shoemaker, in the Butter-market at Bury St Edmunds. He was in apparent good health, chopping a faggot, the same afternoon, when he accidentally cut off one of his fingers, and on his wife's expressing a wish to dress it, he said, 'Never mind, my dear; what is this wound compared to Lord Nelson's?' and immediately fell down in an apoplectic fit, from which he never recovered to answer another sentence.

There is a lovely moment in the second Canto of Dante's Purgatorio *when we are suddenly brought, with the very gentlest of bumps, into the twentieth century – or, indeed, any other century in which the reader may happen to live – and reminded of that other familiar, if fleeting, purgatory of asking other people the way.*

> . . . la nova gente alzo la fronte
> ver noi, dicendo a noi: 'Se voi sapete,
> mostratene la via di gire al monte.'
> E Virgilio rispose: 'Voi credete
> forse che siamo esperti d'esto loco;
> ma noi siam peregrin come voi sete.'

> . . . the new arrivals raised their heads
> towards us: 'If it lies within your power,
> show us the path that leads us to the mount.'
> And Virgil answered: 'Doubtless you believe
> that we are both familiar with this place;
> the trouble is – we're strangers here ourselves.'

Thomas Carlyle on Dante:

Dante does not come before us as a large catholic mind; rather as a narrow and even sectarian mind: it is partly the fruit of his age and position, but partly the fruit of his own nature. His greatness has, in all senses, concentrated itself into fiery emphasis and depth. He is world-great not because he is world-wide, but because he is world-deep.

On Shelley:

He always was, and is, a kind of ghastly object: colourless, pallid, tuneless, without health or warmth or vigour; the sound of him shrieky, frosty, as if a ghost were trying to sing to us.

On Wordsworth:

The languid way in which he gives you a handful of numb, unresponsive fingers is very significant.

On Coleridge:

A weak, diffusive, ineffectual man ... Never did I see such apparatus got ready for thinking and so little thought.

And on himself – as depicted in a portrait by Robert Hardman, painted in 1876 and now in the Scottish National Portrait Gallery, Edinburgh:

It seems a man who is in peaceful relation with himself, and fairly satisfied with his position in the universe.

From a letter by Sarah, Lady Lyttelton, written from St Petersburg on 12 December 1813:

... All the *beau monde* does not walk; many are the ladies who maintain that the said exercise is very pernicious; they accordingly almost lose the use of their legs; and t'other day, as I was going about shopping with Madame Palianski, I observed her footman not only helped her out of the carriage but followed her upstairs, holding her under both elbows as she lounged up. I was making my progress a little more independently, and as soon as she perceived this, '*Mais comment donc! Vous ne vous faîtes pas soutenir? Vous montez toute seule comme cela?*' she exclaimed, quite as if she had found out that I had three legs. And this a lively, healthy little woman of thirty-five!

Here, from Kipling's Debits and Credits, *is the ending of his short story* 'The Gardener'. *A woman is wandering through a military cemetery, looking for the grave of the illegitimate son she has never acknowledged:*

A man knelt behind a line of headstones – evidently a gardener, for he was firming a young plant in the soft earth. She went towards him, her paper in her hand. He rose at her approach and without prelude or salutation asked: 'Who are you looking for?'

'Lieutenant Michael Turrell – my nephew,' said Helen slowly and word for word, as she had many thousands of times in her life.

The man lifted his eyes and looked at her with infinite compassion before he turned from the fresh-sown grass toward the naked black crosses.

'Come with me,' he said, 'and I will show you where your son lies.'

When Helen left the cemetery she turned for a last look. In the distance she saw the man bending over his young plants; and she went away, supposing him to be the gardener.

The all-important reference is to John xx:15.

At Wimpole Hall in Cambridgeshire you may still see the glorious library designed by James Gibbs in 1730 to house some of the 50,000 volumes belonging to Edward Harley, 2nd Earl of Oxford – the finest collection of its time in England. Harley's close friend, the poet Matthew Prior, stayed frequently at Wimpole, where he paid his host the nicest compliment a bibliophile could ever receive:

> Fame counting thy books, my dear Harley, shall tell
> No man had so many who knew them so well.

It was sad that Prior never saw the Gibbs library, having died – in the house, as it happened – in 1721; and sadder still that almost the entire collection, which also included 41,000 prints and some 300,000 pamphlets, was sold by Harley's widow after his death in 1741. (Fortunately she kept back the manuscripts, which were bought twelve years later for the British Museum and form the magnificent Harleian Collection.)

Not many of us can boast what Prior claimed for Harley; we can all, however, take comfort from Disraeli, who wrote to Lady Bradford in August 1878:

> You asked me where I generally lived. In my workshop [i.e. his study] in the morning and always in the library in the evening. Books are companions even if you don't open them.

From the section on the Old Ashmolean – now a museum of the history of science – in The Oxford Guide to Oxford, *by Peter Heyworth:*

The most arresting display is of the equipment used early in the Second World War to develop a technology for the production of penicillin. It is constructed of an assortment of bedpans and old tins – biscuit tins, coffee tins (Lyons pure ground) and one labelled 'Agricultural anti-stomach-and-lung-worm fluid in sheep and lambs'; the control panel (c. 1940) of the counter current penicillin extraction apparatus ('As the resevoir [*sic*] bottles of solvent, crude penicillin, and acid emptied, the relevent [*sic*] lamp on the panel lit and the bell rang to warn the operator') resembles an over-ambitious door bell. It is pure Heath Robinson and very moving. A Pyrex flask contains one of the original cultures of *Penicillium notatum*, now dried up.

In this also is the little world of man compared, and made more like the Universal (man being the measure of all things) that the four Complexions resemble the four Elements, and the seven Ages of man the seven Planets; whereof our infancy is compared to the Moon, in which we seem only to live and grow, as Plants; the second Age to Mercury, wherein we are taught and instructed; our third Age to Venus, the days of Love, Desire and Vanity; the fourth to the Sun, the strong, flourishing and beautiful Age of man's life; the fifth to Mars, in which we seek honour and victory, and in which our thoughts travel to ambitious ends; the sixth Age is ascribed to Jupiter, in which we begin to take account of our time, judge of ourselves, and grow to the perfection of our understanding; the last and seventh Age to Saturn, wherein our days are sad and overcast, and in which we find by dear and lamentable experience, and by the loss which can never be repaired, that of all our vain passions and affections past, the sorrow only abideth.

Sir Walter Ralegh

Will nobody ravish the dollar?
Why from rape should the rouble have rest?
Is there no wily Turk who will furtively lurk
And poke the peseta with zest?
Must the peso remain unpolluted?
Is the lust for the lira quite dead?
Will none, for a lark, take the mark in the park,
Or grapple the guilder in bed?
I fear that I speak with some frankness,
But why should Britannia be mocked,
With pengos and francs lying virgin in banks
While sterling's eternally blocked?

Horace Walpole writes to his friend George Montagu after a visit to Blenheim:

We went to Blenheim, and saw all Vanbrugh's quarries, all the acts of parliament and Gazettes on the Duke in inscriptions, and all the old flock chairs, wainscot tables, and gowns and petticoats of Queen Anne, that old Sarah could crowd among blocks of marble. It looks like the palace of an auctioneer, who has been chosen King of Poland, and furnished his apartments with obsolete trophies, rubbish that nobody bid for, and a dozen pictures, that he had stolen from the inventories of different families. The place is as ugly as the house, and the bridge, like the beggars at the old duchess's gate, begs for a drop of water, and is refused.

Lytton Strachey wrote of Walpole:

His writing, as he might have said himself, is like lace; the material is of very little consequence, the embroidery is all that counts; and it shares with lace the happy faculty of coming out sometimes in yards and yards.

St Augustine's definition of friendship:

To talk and laugh with mutual concessions, to read pleasant books; to jest and to be solemn, to dissent from each other without offence, to teach one another somewhat, or somewhat to learn – to expect those absent with impatience and embrace their return with joy.

It is five years since we have had a really good phrase-book conversation. Here is one from A Guide to Modern Greek, *by E. M. Geldart, published in London in 1873. (I omit the parallel Greek text.)*

– My other luggage I will take with me. That is to say, a foot-wrapper, a stick, three or four parcels, a gun, a lap-dog, two Turkish pipes, and a live tortoise.

– As for the rest, let them pass; but for the dog a separate ticket must be taken, and he must go in the van. As for the tortoise, you must leave that behind: we don't convey vermin!

– Vermin! So you reckon a tortoise among the vermin?

– Certainly, sir. It's an insect.

– An insect! My good fellow, where did you go to school (study)? I refer you to the Zoological Garden(s), and there you will learn, if you have any brains in your head, that the tortoise is a four-footed reptile, and that insects are all six-footed. There's a shilling for you, the price of admission to the Zoological Gardens, except on Mondays, when it is only sixpence. If you have time on Mondays, go twice, that you may be more thoroughly enlightened.

– Oh, that alters the question, sir! And, now I come to think of it, the landlord over the way has a book with those kind of creatures in it. I daresay you're right (*lit.* let be then). All the same, four-foot and six-foot have another meaning in my business.

– All the better! Mind your own business then, and leave the four-footed reptiles to me.

– What place have you taken?

– Third class.

– Why do you travel third?

– Because there's no fourth.

– There is in Ireland, however.

– Yes, indeed; there are many strange things in Ireland. Four classes (orders), and no order – at least, great disorder.

– Is there better order to be found in Greece?

– You will see.

– Strange fellows, these English; but they eat well, and they pay well.

– What did you say?

– I said, we always know the English by their ready wit and their excellent French pronunciation.

– But my friend is a Greek.

– We admire the Greeks too. They were the Frenchmen of antiquity.

In St Mary's church at Wraxall, Dorset, is a monument to a certain William Lawrence. It bears the inscription:

Welcome dear death let sweetest sleep here take me
In thy cool shades and never more awake mee
Like a rich cortege draw thy darkness round
Like a closed Chamber make my grave profound
In it I'le couch secure no dreames affright
A silent lodger here no cares dare bite
Making thy bed seeme hard or long thy night
Let not thy armes Oh grave yet still enfold mee
Alas think not thou canst for ever hold mee
Wee'le breake at length thy marble wombe asunder
Reissue thence and fill the world with wonder
Envy thou'll then to see the Power divine
Nevre digge his Diamonds from thy deepest myne
Cleanse cleare and polish them then shall by farre
Each dust of theirs outshine the morning starre.

The date is given as 1681.

Another inscription, at Kempsey in Worcestershire, commemorates one George Boulter, who served as vicar there for thirty years, and the two wives who predeceased him in 1757 and 1774 respectively. 'He died,' we are told, 'January 30th, aged 81' – but the year is not disclosed.

Underneath the corruptible Parts of a Vicar, one Husband, two Helpmeets, both Wives, and both ANNs, a Triplicity of Persons in two Twains, but one Flesh, are interred.

WITH A GIFT OF RINGS

It was no costume jewellery I sent:
True stones cool to the tongue, their settings ancient,
Their magic evident.
Conceal your pride, accept them negligently
But, naked on your couch, wear them for me.

Robert Graves

The 1973 Cracker contained the first part of a splendid diatribe by Ruskin against the architect Augustus Welby Pugin for 'being lured into the Romanist Church by the glitter of it, like larks into a trap by broken glass'. I came across the passage again the other day (you will find it in Appendix 12 to Vol. I of the first edition of The Stones of Venice) *and can't resist quoting a bit more. This second salvo is directed against a passage from Pugin's 'Remarks', in which he wrote:*

I believe, as regards architecture, few men have been so unfortunate as myself ... I have never had the chance of producing a single fine ecclesiastical building, except my own church ... but everything else, either for want of adequate funds or injudicious interference and control, or some other contingency, is more or less a failure ... St George's was spoilt by the very instructions laid down by the committee, that it was to hold 3,000 people on the floor at a limited price; in consequence height, proportion, everything, was sacrificed to meet these conditions ...

For Ruskin, that was enough:

Is that so? Phidias can niche himself into the corner of a pediment, and Raffaelle expatiate within the circumference of a clay platter, but Pugin is inexpressible in less than a cathedral. Let his ineffableness be assured of this, once and for all, that no difficulty or restraint ever happened to a man of real power, but his power was the more manifested in the contending with or conquering it; and that there is no field so small, no cranny so contracted, but that a great spirit can house and manifest itself therein. The thunder that smites the Alp into dust, can gather itself into the width of a golden wire. Whatever greatness there was in you, had it been Buonarroti's own, you had room enough for it in a single niche; you might have put the whole power of it into two feet cube of Caen stone. St George's was not high enough for want of money? But was it want of money that made you put that blunt, overloaded, laborious ogee door into the side of it? Was it for lack of funds that you sunk the tracing of the parapet in its clumsy zigzags? Was it parsimony that you buried its paltry pinnacles in that eruption of diseased crockets? Or in pecuniary embarrassment that you set up the belfry fools' caps with the mimicry of dormer windows which nobody can reach nor look out of? Not so, but in more incapability of better things ...

I am sorry to have to speak thus of any living architect ... He has a most sincere love for his profession, a heartily honest enthusiasm of pyxes and piscinas; and though he will never design so much as a pyx or a piscina thoroughly well, yet better than most of the experimental architects of the day. Employ him by all means, but on small work. Expect no cathedrals of him; but no one at present can design a better finial.

Poor Pugin: no wonder that within weeks of the publication of the above he was confined to Bedlam, where he died the following year. A contrite Ruskin withdrew the whole passage from the second edition.

In the Plaza de las Tres Culturas in Mexico City we can still see the remains of the old Aztec centre of Tlatelolco; beside them stand a magnificent Spanish colonial church and a soaring skyscraper. A plaque in the centre of the square bears an inscription. It reads:

El 13 de Agosto de 1521
Heroicamente defendido por Cuauhtemoc
Cayo Tlatelolco en poder de Hernan Cortés.
Ne fue triunfo ni derrota
Fue el doloroso nacimiento del pueblo mestizo
Que es el Mexico de hoy.

On 13 August 1521
Heroically defended by Cuauhtemoc
Tlatelolco fell to the might of Hernan Cortés.
It was neither a triumph nor a defeat
It was the painful birth of the commingled people
That is the Mexico of today.

The things people write under 'Recreation' in their Who's Who *entries are usually far more boring than they should be. Reading, golf, gardening, squash – the tired old pastimes come up again and again. Then, just occasionally, the monotony is shattered. Here are a few examples, culled from various recent editions:*

Charles Causley: The rediscovery of his native town [Launceston]. Playing the piano with expression.

John Faulkner: Intricacies and wildernesses.

John Fowles: Mainly Sabine.

Bevis Hillier: Awarding marks out of ten for suburban front gardens.

James Kirkup: Standing in shafts of moonlight.

Edward Lucie-Smith: Walking the dog; malice.

Frederic Raphael: Painting things white.

Constant Hendrick [now Sir Henry] de Waal: Remaining (so far as possible) unaware of current events.

Keith Waterhouse: Lunch.

Professor Roy Worskett: Looking and listening in disbelief.

Best of all was the 1980 entry – now, alas, deleted – by Sir Harold Hobson:

Bridge; recollecting in regretful tranquillity the magical things and people I may never see again – the Grand Véfour, Lasserre, Beaumanière; Proust's Grand Hotel at Balbec (Cabourg); Sunday afternoon teas at the Ritz; the theatrical bookshop in St Germain-des-Prés; the Prado; Edwige Feuillère, Madeleine Renauld, Jean-Louis Barrault, François Perier; collecting from ephemera of the Belle Epoque the cartoons of Steinlen; and always and inexhaustibly talking to my wife.

It was my friend Peter Levi who introduced me to the Davideis, *a marvellous poem by Abraham Cowley (1618–67) – much of it written while he was still an undergraduate at Cambridge. Here is an extract:*

When *Gabriel*, (no blest *Spirit* more kind and fair)
Bodies and Cloaths himself with thicken'd Air,
All like a comely *Youth* in life's fresh Bloom,
Rare Workmanship, and wrought by heav'nly Loom!
He took for a Skin a Cloud most soft and bright,
That e'er the mid-day Sun pierced through with Light:
Upon his Cheeks a lively Blush he spread,
Washed from the Morning Beauties deepest Red.
An harmless flaming *Meteor* shone for Hair,
And fell adown his Shoulders with loose Care.
He cuts out a silk *Mantle* from the Skies,
Where the most sprightly Azure pleased the Eyes.
This he with starry Vapours spangles all,
Took in their Prime e'er they grow *ripe*, and *fall.*
Of a new Rainbow e'er it fret or fade,
The choicest Piece took out, a *Scarf* is made.
Small streaming Clouds he does for Wings display,
Not virtuous Lovers Sighs more soft than they.
These he gilds o'er with the Sun's richest Rays,
Caught gliding o'er pure Streams on which he plays.
    Thus dress'd, the joyful *Gabriel* posts away,
    And carries with him his own glorious Day . . .

Reading this, one is not altogether surprised to learn that Milton named Cowley as being the living poet he most admired. 'Mr Dryden,' he said, 'is only a versifier.'

Charles Evans of Heinemann's loved to tell the story of how one day, for want of any other conversational gambit, he complimented the wife of Francis Brett Young on the stockings that her husband was wearing with his plus-fours. Mrs Brett Young immediately offered to knit him some; later, however, there arrived a parcel, containing a remarkably worn and threadbare pair with a covering note:

Dear Charles,

I'm sorry I haven't had time to knit you those stockings. Instead, I'm sending you these, which I thought you might like to have as they are the ones in which Francis wrote *Dr Bradley Remembers*.

Yours sincerely,
Jessica Brett Young.

Who are these from the strange ineffable places,
From the Topaze Mountain and Desert of Doubt,
With the glow of the Yemen full on their faces
And a breath from the spices of Hadramaut?

Travel-apprentices, travel indenturers,
Young men, old men, black hair, white,
Names to conjure with, wild adventurers,
From the noonday furnace and purple night.

Burckhardt, Halévy, Niebuhr, Slater,
Seventeenth, eighteenth-century bays,
Seetzen, Sadleir, Struys, and later
Down to the long Victorian days.

A thousand miles at the back of Aden,
There they had time to think of things,
In the outer silence and burnt air laden
With the shadow of death and a vulture's wings.

There they remembered the last house in Samna,
Last of the plane-trees, last shepherd and flock,
Prayed for the heavens to rain down manna,
Prayed for a Moses to strike the rock.

Famine and fever flagged their forces
Till they died in a dream of ice and fruit,
In the long-forgotten watercourses
By the edge of Queen Zobeïde's route.

They have left the hope of the green oases,
The fear of the bleaching bones and the pest,
They have found the more ineffable places –
Allah has given them rest.

John Meade Falkner
(1858–1932)

How curious that the author of such a poem should have been compiler of Murray's Handbooks to Oxfordshire and Berkshire. But he was more. Anthony Hobson tells me that he retired from being chairman of Armstrong Whitworth* *to become honorary liturgiologist to the Dean and Chapter of Durham.*

---

* '*A position in which he can hardly be called a success*' (D.N.B.).

Having bought the colours, an easel, and a canvas, the next step was *to begin*. But what a step to take! The palette gleamed with beads of colour; fair and white rose the canvas; the empty brush hung poised, heavy with destiny, irresolute in the air. My hand seemed arrested by a silent veto. But after all the sky on this occasion was unquestionably blue, and a pale blue at that. There could be no doubt that blue paint mixed with white should be put on the top part of the canvas. One really does not need to have had an artist's training to see that. It is a starting-point open to all. So very gingerly I mixed a little blue paint on the palette with a very small brush, and then with infinite precaution made a mark about as big as a bean upon the affronted snow-white shield. It was a challenge, a deliberate challenge; but so subdued, so halting, indeed so cataleptic, that it deserved no response. At that moment the loud approaching sound of a motor-car was heard in the drive. From this chariot there stepped swiftly and lightly none other than the gifted wife of Sir John Lavery. 'Painting! But what are you hesitating about? Let me have a brush – the big one.' Splash into the turpentine, wallop into the blue and the white, frantic flourish on the palette – clean no longer – and then several large, fierce strokes and splashes of blue on the absolutely cowering canvas. Anyone could see that it could not hit back. No evil fate avenged the jaunty violence. The canvas grinned in helplessness before me. The spell was broken. The sickly inhibitions rolled away. I seized the largest brush and fell upon my victim with berserk fury. I have never felt any awe of a canvas since.

When the conversation turned to painting, there was one particular poem that he loved to recite. Imagine, if you can, the delivery in that unique Churchillian French:

> La peinture à l'huile
> Est bien difficile;
> Mais c'est beaucoup plus beau
> Que la peinture à l'eau.

And the best and the worst of this is
That neither is more to blame
If you have forgotten my kisses
And I have forgotten your name.

Swinburne

*One of my favourite Elizabethan poets is Samuel Daniel – author of the
sonnet to sleep which I included in the 1978 Cracker. (Ben Jonson said that
he was no poet at all, but I can't help that.) Here is his imagined dialogue
between Ulysses and the Siren:*

SYREN: Come worthy Greeke, *Ulisses* come
      Possesse these shores with me:
      The windes and Seas are troublesome,
      And heere we may be free.
        Here may we sit, and view their toile
      That travaile in the deepe,
      And joy the day in mirth the while,
      And spend the night in sleepe.

ULISSES: Faire Nimph, if fame, or honour were
      To be attayned with ease,
      Then would I come, and rest with thee,
      And leave such toiles as these.
        But here it dwels, and here must I
      With danger seeke it forth,
      To spend the time luxuriously
      Becomes not men of worth.

SYREN: *Ulisses*, O be not deceiv'd
      With that unreall name:
      This honour is a thing conceiv'd,
      And rests on others' fame.
        Begotten onely to molest
      Our peace, and to beguile
      (The best thing of our life) our rest,
      And give us up to toile.

ULISSES: Delicious Nimph, suppose there were
      Nor honour, nor report,
      Yet manlines would scorne to weare
      The time in idle sport.
        For toyle doth give a better touch,
      To make us feele our joy;
      And ease findes tediousnesse as much
      As labour yeelds annoy.

SYREN: Then pleasure likewise seemes the shore,
      Whereto tends all your toyle,
      Which you forego to make it more,
      And perish oft the while.

Who may disporte them diversly,
Finde never tedious day,
And ease may have varietie,
As well as action may.

ULISSES: But natures of the noblest frame
These toyles, and dangers please,
And they take comfort in the same,
As much as you in ease.
And with the thought of actions past
Are recreated still;
When pleasure leaves a touch at last
To shew that it was ill.

SYREN: That doth opinion onely cause,
That's out of custome bred,
Which makes us many other lawes
Than ever Nature did.
No widdowes waile for our delights,
Our sportes are without bloud,
The world we see by warlike wights
Receives more hurt than good.

ULISSES: But yet the state of things require
These motions of unrest,
And these great Spirits of high desire
Seeme borne to turne them best.
To purge the mischiefes that increase,
And all good order mar:
For oft we see a wicked peace
To be well changed for war.

SYREN: Well, well *Ulisses* then I see,
I shall not have thee heere,
And therefore I will come to thee,
And take my fortunes there.
I must be wonne that cannot win,
Yet lost were I not wonne:
For beauty hath created bin,
T'undoo, or be undonne.

A Christmas Cracker

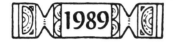

For the past eighty years I have started each day in the same manner. It is not a mechanical routine but something essential to my daily life. I go to the piano, and I play two preludes and fugues of Bach. I cannot think of doing otherwise. It is a sort of benediction on the house. But that is not its only meaning for me. It is a rediscovery of the world of which I have the joy of being a part. It fills me with awareness of the wonder of life, with a feeling of the incredible marvel of being human.

Pablo Casals,
at the age of ninety-three

When Pamela Egremont returned a year or two ago from Peking, she brought back a copy of the following circular which she kindly passed on to me. It was typed entirely in capital letters.

FROM EMBASSY OF THE REPUBLIC OF SIERRA LEONE
PEKING

THIS IS TO INFORM ALL MISSIONS HERE ESPECIALLY THE WIVES OF OTHER DIPLOMATS HERE IN PEKING OF THE INCIDENT SURROUNDING THE SUDDEN DEPARTURE FROM PEKING OF THE SIERRA LEONE AMBASSADOR'S WIFE MRS THERESA MALOMO KOJO RANDALL.

MRS KOJO RANDALL LEFT PEKING SUDDENLY TO AVOID SCANDALL AFTER THE HUSBAND CAUGHT HER WITH A PACKET OF POISON WHICH WAS SUPPOSEDLY SENT TO HER BY HER GUINEAN SWEETHEART WHOM SHE ALREADY HAS A 1 YEAR OLD SON FOR AND FROM WHOM THE AMBASSADOR SNATCHED HER AWAY TO COME TO PEKING. THIS IS THE REASON INFACT WHY HE DID NOT REALISE SHE WAS ALREADY PREGNANT BEFORE HE MARRIED HER AND SHE HAD TO COME AND UNDER GO AN ABORTION HERE IN PEKING ON HER ARRIVAL.

THE POISON WAS SUPPOSED TO BE USED IN COOKING FOOD FOR THE AMBASSADOR TO KILL HIM SO THAT MRS RANDALL CAN EASILY RETURN TO HER GUINEAN TRADER SWEETHEART IN FREETOWN.

WELL INFORMED SOURCES IN FREETOWN SAID MRS RANDALL CONFESSED IN SIERRA LEONE THAT SHE WAS ADVISED TO SEND FOR AND USE THE POISON FOR HER HUSBAND BY THE WIFE OF THE FIRST SECRETARY OF THE EMBASSY MRS STELLA SAQUEE WHO CLAIMED A VAST EXPERIENCE IN USING SUCH JUJU (WITCHCRAFT) TO KEEP HER OWN HUSBAND QUIET THIS IS WAY HE DOES NOT NOTICE THAT SHE SLEEPS AROUND WITH A LOT OF MEN HERE IN PEKING.

ALL DIPLOMATIC MISSION
PEKING

In February 1972, my mother celebrated her eightieth birthday (six months early, it must be said) by taking several of her family and friends on an African safari. While we were away, her beloved miniature chihuahua – always known as Doggie – breathed his last. I was determined not to spoil her holiday, so did not tell her until five minutes before we got home.

A few days later, her friend Sir Colin Anderson sent her the following:

EPITAPH FOR A VERY SMALL DOG

Diana's dear, her constant *DOG*, has died:
Who earned no envy, for he showed no pride;
Though, as the cynosure of all men's eyes,
Some may have wished to cut him down to size.
A silly aim – he had no size to spare –
Yet jealousy makes idiots, everywhere.
Diana's moon, the brightest of the bright,
Now he is gone, has lost her lovely light;
Her smuggling sleeve now mourns its weightless cuff;
And lonely droops her kennel-worthy muff.
No longer shall we meet his limpid eyes,
Passing, it seemed, old Aztec messages;
No longer watch him glide on twinkling feet
With insect speed along the lamp-lit street,
And then return, drawn back from out the gloom,
By the sweet promise of Diana's room.

Polite in life – in death all chivalry,
He spared his Mistress what she should not see.
'Death must be private; loved one far away . . .'
So *DOGGIE* said – and who shall say him nay?

Two pretty pieces of Nelsoniana. The first is a remark made by Captain William Pringle, R.N., to one of his brother-officers on 12 March 1787, the day after Nelson's wedding in the West Indies:

The Navy, Sir, yesterday lost one of its greatest ornaments, by Nelson's marriage. It is a national loss, that such an officer should marry: had it not been for that circumstance, I foresee that Nelson would become the greatest man in the Service.

His wife was the widow of Dr Nisbet of Nevis, by whom she had a small son. On 17 December 1794, during a brief absence from Burnham Thorpe – where they were living with Nelson's father – she wrote to her husband:

My child I figure to myself good, obedient to you, and I hope tells you all the secrets of his heart. If he does you will keep him good. Do make him clean his teeth not cross ways but upwards and downwards.

When my daughter Artemis was preparing her recent book Cairo in the War, *she discovered the wartime letters of our beloved and much-missed friend Charles Johnston, who has already appeared in the 1986* Cracker. (*He was to go on to be Ambassador in Amman and Governor of Aden.*) *Here is one of them, addressed to his mother and dated 29 May 1943:*

Cairo.

The Arabic exam was rather amusing. It was held in the Sudan Agency, which is the local office of the Sudan Govt and has an atmosphere of its own. You walk out of an ordinary Cairo street, that's to say from surroundings which aren't really oriental or tropical at all but are more like a hotter, dingier, provincial version of Paris, into a large, cool office which might have been brought straight from Khartoum as it stood – with none of the plush and gilding and pseudo-Empire furniture of an Egyptian Government office, but with bare tiles and bare green-distempered walls, hung here and there with heads of wild animals and very old photographs of trains and river-steamers which were obviously frightfully modern once. You have the impression very strongly of what is called 'the Khartoum atmosphere' – of a very efficient nineteenth-century empire run by old Wykehamists in big bare offices where the windows and shutters are always closed to keep the heat out, and fans are whirring and there is a strong smell of 'flit'.

The exam was run with typical Sudan Service efficiency . . . very exactly regulated by Ted Sanders (the Sudan Agent and, needless to say, a Wykehamist) with papers and marks and time limits and an impressive oral exam, in which an enormous black man, who obviously came from the wrong side of Wadi Halfa and spoke an entirely different dialect from my sophisticated Coptic, Cairene, café-sitting professor, was brought in and gabbled something sheepishly with a huge hot potato in his mouth. After making him repeat it six times, I at last got the sense of it: the station master had telephoned to say that the Ambassador's train was half an hour late and would I tell the Private Secretary and the A.D.C.

Fortunately our Arabic exam moves in a very closed world . . . of Anglo-Egyptian officialdom before the last war, and you can't go far wrong so long as you know the Arabic for special train, red carpet, A.D.C., duck-shooting, G.O.C. British troops, Assistant Oriental Secretary, Inspector General of Irrigation, and the Gezira Sporting Club (which we call Gezira and the Egyptians 'El Zborting').

Adam Watson and I passed, but poor old Peter Stirling was ploughed . . . the standard of the exam is pretty low, but it's unfortunately gone up since the time when a candidate was asked to make a non-English-speaking Egyptian understand that the King of Iraq had been killed in a motor crash. The candidate did not know any Arabic to speak of, but he did know that *malik* meant king, so he said: '*Malik el Iraq fi automobile – boomp, boomp – finish malik*', and the Egyptian understood and he passed with flying colours.

I always used to think that there was only one French limerick worthy of the name – the one that went

Il y avait une personne de Dijon
Qui n'aimait pas trop la religion;
   Il disait 'Ma foi!
   Ils m'emmerdent tous les trois –
Et le père, et le fils, et le pigeon.'

But I know now that I was wrong, Ken Davison having furnished me with two more, which I have since learnt were written by Edward Gorey:

Les salons de la ville de Trieste
Sont vaseux, suraigus et funestes;
   Parmi les grandes chaises
   On cause de malaises,
Des estropiements et des pestes.

Un moine, au milieu de la messe,
S'éleva et cria en détresse:
   'La vie religieuse
   Est sale et affreuse!'
Et se poignarda entre les fesses.

while Pat Gibson, not to be outdone, proposes:

Il était un gendarme, à Nanteuil,
Qui n'avait qu'une dent et qu'un oeil;
   Mais cet oeil solitaire
   Etait plein de mystère,
Cette dent, d'importance et d'orgueil.

I have recently discovered that the author of the above was none other than Sir George du Maurier who, I learn from the Dictionary of National Biography, *wrote vers de société with equal elegance in both French and English. I suspect that he was also responsible for the following. In the first – which I recently noticed beneath his portrait in the loo of the Garrick Club – he would have been writing his own obituary; but perhaps the second was his* chef d'oeuvre.

L'artiste du *Punch*, feu du Maurier,
Moissonnait un beau tas de lauriers;
   Et de nos jours son fils
   Dans les rangs de Thespis
S'est établi au front – et encore y
   est!

Un vieux duc (le meilleur
   des époux)
Demanda, en lui tâtant le pouls,
   A sa vieille duchesse
   Qu'un vieux catarrhe oppresse,
'Et ton thé, t'a-t-il ôté ta toux?'

Mr Molineux,

Few words are best. My letters to my father have come to the eyes of some. Neither can I condemn any but you for it. If it be so, you have played the very knave with me; and so I will make you know, if I have good proof of it. But that for so much as is past. For that is to come, I assure you before God, that if ever I know you do so much as read any letter I write to my father without his commandment, or my consent, I will thrust my dagger into you. And trust to it, for I speak it in earnest. In the meantime, farewell.

One of the most attractive characteristics of Alexander the Great was his love of Homer. His biographer Robin Lane Fox, who shares that love to the full, explains it thus:

For of all poems, Homer's *Iliad* is still the most immediate, a world whose reality never falters, not only as seen through the new dimension of its similes, where kings banquet beneath their oak trees, children build castles of sand, mothers keep flies away from their sleeping babies and old women watch from their porches as the wedding processions dance by, but also through the leisurely progress of a narrative rich in ritual and repeated phrases, deceptively simple but infinitely true, where heroes strive for glory knowing that death is inescapable, where a white-armed lady laughs through her tears and returns to heat the bath-water for a husband who she knows will never return from the battle, where gods and goddesses are no more remote for being powerful, one raining tears of blood for the death of a favourite hero, another making toys, another bribing Sleep with the promise of one of the younger Graces and then making love with Zeus her husband on a carpet of crocus and hyacinth. Homer's only magic is his own, and if he still speaks directly to the heart how much more must his poems have come home to Alexander, who saw their ideals around him and chose to live them, not as a distant reader but more in the spirit of a marcher baron living out the ballads which mirrored his own home world.

With the single exception of Homer, there is no eminent writer, not even Sir Walter Scott, whom I can despise so entirely as I despise Shakespeare when I measure my mind against his.

George Bernard Shaw

THE HORSES

Barely a twelvemonth after
The seven days' war that put the world to sleep,
Late in the evening the strange horses came.
By then we had made our covenant with silence,
But in the first few days it was so still
We listened to our breathing and were afraid.
On the second day
The radios failed; we turned the knobs; no answer.
On the third day a warship passed us, heading north,
Dead bodies piled on the deck. On the sixth day
A plane plunged over us into the sea. Thereafter
Nothing. The radios dumb;
And still they stand in corners of our kitchens,
And stand, perhaps, turned on, in a million rooms
All over the world. But now if they should speak,
If on a sudden they should speak again,
If on the stroke of noon a voice should speak,
We would not listen, we would not let it bring
That old bad world that swallowed its children quick
At one great gulp. We would not have it again.
Sometimes we think of the nations lying asleep,
Curled blindly in impenetrable sorrow,
And then the thought confounds us with its strangeness.
The tractors lie about our fields; at evening
They look like dank sea-monsters couched and waiting.
We leave them where they are and let them rust:
'They'll moulder away and be like other loam.'
We make our oxen drag our rusty ploughs
Long laid aside. We have gone back
Far past our fathers' land.
    And then, that evening,
Late in the summer the strange horses came.
We heard a distant tapping on the road,
A deepening drumming; it stopped, went on again
And at the corner changed to hollow thunder.
We saw the heads
Like a wild wave charging and were afraid.
We had sold our horses in our fathers' time
To buy new tractors. Now they were strange to us

As fabulous steeds set on an ancient shield
Or illustrations in a book of knights.
We did not dare go near them. Yet they waited,
Stubborn and shy, as if they had been sent
By an old command to find our whereabouts
And that long-lost archaic companionship.
In the first moment we had never a thought
That they were creatures to be owned and used.
Among them were some half-a-dozen colts
Dropped in some wilderness of the broken world,
Yet new as if they had come from their own Eden.
Since then they have pulled our ploughs and borne our loads,
But that free servitude still can pierce our hearts.
Our life is changed; their coming our beginning.

Edwin Muir

In February 1865 the Speaker of the House of Commons dined with the Prime Minister, Lord Palmerston, then eighty. The Speaker told Disraeli that Palmerston 'ate for dinner two plates of turtle soup; he was then served very amply to a plate of cod and oyster sauce; he then took a *pâté*; afterwards he was helped to two very greasy-looking *entrées*; he then despatched a plate of roast mutton; then there appeared before him the largest, and to my mind the hardest, slice of ham that ever figured on the table of a nobleman, yet it disappeared, just in time for him to answer the inquiry of his butler: "Snipe, my Lord, or pheasant?" He instantly replied pheasant, thus completing his ninth dish of meat at that meal.'

Disraeli's Reminiscences, *1865*

Two more dictionary definitions:

Mallemaroking: 1867. *Smith Taylor's Word-Book.* The visiting and carousing of seamen in the Greenland ships.

[O.E.D]

Taghairm: *n.* In the Scottish Highlands, divination: *esp.* inspiration sought by lying in a bullock's hide beneath a waterfall.

[Chambers]

And two of those selected quotations, included in the better dictionaries in order to illustrate the use of the word defined. The first clearly struck a deep chord of sympathy in the soul of the lexicographer; it comes from the Oxford English Dictionary, *as part of the entry for the word* Scriptorium:

TLS, 18 January 1907: Drowsy intelligences and numbed fingers in a draughty scriptorium will easily account for deviations.

The source of the second is a Norwegian–English dictionary by Professor Einar Haugen (Universitetsforlaget, Oslo, 1965)*:*

Kanskje: Perhaps, maybe ... *Kanskje blir vi ferdig med denne ordboken en gang* – Maybe we'll finish this dictionary some time.

In the Cathedral of Bury St Edmunds is a tombstone that reads:

Reader
Pause at this Humble Stone
it Records
The fall of unguarded Youth
By the allurements of vice
and the treacherous snares
of Seduction
SARAH LLOYD
on the 23d. of April 1800
in the 22d. Year of her Age
Suffered a Just but ignominious
DEATH
for admitting her abandoned seducer
into the Dwelling-House of
her Mistress
in the Night of 3d Oct
1799
and becoming the Instrument
in his Hands of the crimes
of Robbery and House-burning
These were her last Words
May my example be a
warning to Thousands.

Paul Scott's The Raj Quartet *seems to me to be one of the major literary achievements of our century. The following passage – which comes from the first of the four volumes,* The Jewel in the Crown *– is as strong and spare as the idol it describes:*

There are trees in the courtyard. In the day they afford some shade. Behind the main sanctuary is the sanctuary of the sleeping Vishnu. The stone of the sanctuary floor is rubbed black and shiny. Inside, in the dim light of the oil-lamps set in the walls, the carved recumbent god sleeps through an eternity of what look like pleasant dreams. He is longer than a lying man would be. He is part of his own stone pallet, carved into it, out of it, inseparable from it. He is smooth and naked, with square shoulders and full lips that curve at the corners into a smile. The eyelids are shut but seem always to be on the point of fluttering voluptuously open. Once this imminent awakening has made its impression, the stiff limbs begin to suggest a hidden flexibility as though, at last, the god may be expected to ease the cramp of long sleep out of them. The delicately carved but powerful hand would then drop from the stone pillow and fall aslant the breast. And then perhaps the full lips would part and he would speak one word, speaking it softly, as in a dream, but revealing a secret that would enable whatever man or woman happened to be there to learn the secret of power on earth or peace beyond it.

Thomas Jefferson, writing to the Rev. Isaac Story on 5 December 1801 about the after life:

When I was young I was fond of the speculations which seemed to promise some insight into that hidden country, but observing at length that they left me in the same ignorance in which they had found me, I have for very many years ceased to read or to think concerning them, and have reposed my head on that pillow of ignorance which a benevolent Creator has made so soft for us, knowing how much we should be forced to use it.

My own feelings exactly.

In Augustus Hare's autobiography, The Story of My Life, *he tells a splendid tale of how, when attacked by brigands in Naples in 1881 or 1882, he managed to limit the damage by appealing to their snobbery:*

At Naples, returning at night from the hotels in the lower town to those on the ridge of the hill, a gentleman engaged me in conversation and strolled along by my side. Suddenly, in the most desolate part of the road, he blew a whistle, and another man leapt out of the bushes, and both rushing upon me demanded '*L'orologio e la borsa.*' [Your watch and purse.] I declared that I had neither watch nor purse. They insisted on my turning out all my pockets, which contained only three francs in paper and sixteen soldi in copper. Then they demanded my ring. I refused, and said it was no use for them to try to get it; it had not been off my finger for more than thirty years: it would not come off. They struggled to get it off, but could not. Then they whispered together. I said, 'I see what you mean to do: you mean to cut off my finger and then drop me into the sea (which there – opposite the Boschetto – is deep water); but remember, I shall be missed and looked for.' – 'No, we took good care to ascertain that first,' said my first acquaintance; 'you said you had only been two days in Naples (and so I had): people who have been only two days in Naples are never missed.' – 'But I do know Naples well – *bisogna esaminarmi sopra Napoli,*' [You must ask me about Naples] I protested. '*Dunque chi fu la Principessa Altamonti?*' – '*Fu figlia del Conte Cini di Roma, sorella della Duchessa Cirella.*' [She is the daughter of Count Cini of Rome and the sister of the Duchess Cirella.] – '*E chi è il Principe S. Teodoro?*' [And who is Prince San Teodoro?] – '*Fu Duca di S. Arpino, si maritava con una signora Inglese, Lady Burghersh, chi sta adesso Lady Walsingham.*' [He is the Duke of San Arpino, who married an English lady, Lady Burghersh, who is now Lady Walsingham.] After this they decided to let me go! But the strangest part of all was that the first brigand said, 'After this scene you will not be able to walk home, and a carriage from the *guardia* costs sixty centesimi; therefore that sum I shall give you back,' and they counted twelve soldi from the sum they had taken. It is this fact which makes me speak of the men who attacked me at Naples as brigands, not as robbers.

I have to make a rule not to draw too deeply for these Crackers on the
Notebooks *of Geoffrey Madan, as I might otherwise easily find myself
copying down every entry. Just occasionally, however, the temptation
becomes too great to resist, as with A. C. Benson's observation on Dr
Arnold:*

A man who could burst into tears at his own dinner-table on
hearing a comparison made between St Paul and St John to the
detriment of the latter, and beg that the subject might never be
mentioned again in his presence, could never have been an *easy*
companion.

Rue Saint-Florentin, il y a un palais et un égout.

Le palais, qui est d'une noble, riche et morne architecture, s'est appelé longtemps: *Hôtel de l'Infantado*; aujourd'hui on lit sur le fronton de sa porte principale: Hôtel Talleyrand. Pendant les quarante ans qu'il a habité cette rue, l'hôte dernier de ce palais n'a peut-être jamais laissé tomber son regard sur cet égout.

C'était un personnage étrange, redouté et considérable; il s'appelait Charles-Maurice de Périgord; il était noble comme Machiavel, prêtre comme Gondi, défroqué comme Fouché, spirituel comme Voltaire et boiteux comme le diable. On pourrait dire que tout en lui boitait comme lui; la noblesse qu'il avait faite servante de la république, la prêtrise qu'il avait traînée au Champ de Mars, puis jetée au ruisseau, le mariage qu'il avait rompu par vingt scandales et par une séparation volontaire, l'esprit qu'il déshonorait par la bassesse . . .

Pendant trente ans, du fond de son palais, du fond de sa pensée, il avait à peu près mené l'Europe. Il s'était laissé tutoyer par la révolution et lui avait souri, ironiquement, il est vrai; mais elle ne s'en était pas aperçue. Il avait approché, connu, observé, pénétré, remué, retourné, approfondi, raillé, fécondé, tous les hommes de son temps, toutes les idées de son siècle, et il y avait eu dans sa vie des minutes où, tenant en sa main les quatre ou cinq fils formidables qui faisaient mouvoir l'univers civilisé, il avait pour pantin Napoléon Ier, empereur des Français, roi d'Italie, protecteur de la confédération du Rhin, médiateur de la confédération suisse. Voilà à quoi jouait cet homme . . .

Il avait fait tout cela dans son palais, et, dans ce palais, comme une araignée dans sa toile, il avait successivement attiré et pris héros, penseurs, grands hommes, conquérants, rois, princes, empereurs, Bonaparte, Sieyès, Mme de Staël, Chateaubriand, Benjamin Constant, Alexandre de Russie, Guillaume de Prusse, François d'Autriche, Louis XVIII, Louis-Philippe, toutes les mouches dorées et rayonnantes qui bourdonnent dans l'histoire de ces quarante dernières années. Tout cet étincelant essaim, fasciné par l'oeil profond de cet homme, avait successivement passé sous cette porte sombre qui porte écrit sur son architrave: HOTEL TALLEYRAND.

Eh bien, avant-hier 17 mai 1838, cet homme est mort. Des médecins sont venus et ont embaumé le cadavre. Pour cela, à la manière des Egyptiens, ils ont retiré les entrailles du ventre et le cerveau du crâne. La chose faite, après avoir transformé le prince de Talleyrand en momie et cloué cette momie dans une bière tapissée de satin blanc, ils se sont retirés, laissant sur une table la cervelle, cette cervelle qui avait pensé tant de choses, inspiré tant d'hommes, construit tant d'édifices, conduit deux révolutions, trompé vingt rois, contenu le monde. Les médecins partis, un valet est entré, il a vu ce qu'ils avaient laissé: Tiens! ils ont oublié cela. Qu'en faire? Il s'est souvenu qu'il y avait un égout dans la rue, il y est allé, et a jeté le cerveau dans cet égout. *Finis rerum.*

Victor Hugo

How beautiful, I have often thought, would be the names of many of our vilest diseases, were it not for their disagreeable associations. My old friend Jenny Fraser sends me this admirable illustration of the fact by J. C. Squire:

So forth there rode Sir Erysipelas
From good Lord Goitre's castle, with the steed
Loose on the rein: and, as he rode, he mused
On Knights and Ladies dead: Sir Scrofula,
Sciatica of Glanders and his friend,
Stout Sir Colitis out of Aquitaine,
And Impetigo, proudest of them all,
Who lived and died for blind Queen Cholera's sake:
Anthrax, who dwelt in the enchanted wood
With those princesses three, tall, pale and dumb,
And beautiful, whose names were music's self,
Anaemia, Influenza, Eczema.
And then, once more, the incredible dream came back
How long ago, upon the fabulous shores
Of far Lumbago, all on a summer's day,
He and the maid Neuralgia, they twain,
Lay in a flower-crowned mead, and garlands wove
Of gout, and yellow hydrocephaly,
Dim palsies, and pyrrhoea, and the sweet
Myopia, bluer than the summer sky:
Agues, both white and red, pied common cold,
Cirrhosis, and that wan, faint flower of love
The shepherds call dyspepsia. – Gone! all gone!
There came a Knight: he cried 'Neuralgia!'
And never a voice to answer. Only rang
O'er cliff and battlement and desolate mere
'Neuralgia!' in the echo's mockery.

Of Henry Cavendish, the celebrated physicist, it was said by Lord Brougham – who knew him as well as anyone – that 'he probably uttered fewer words in the course of his life than any man who ever lived to fourscore years, not at all excepting the monks of La Trappe.' Jim Lees-Milne calls my attention to an anecdote taken from The Life Story of William Herschel and his Sister Caroline Herschel, *edited by his grand-daughter Constance A. Lubbock, 1933. It should perhaps be explained that before the days of the great astronomer stars were always thought to have tails or points, just as we still tend to draw them today.*

At a dinner given by Mr Aubert in the year 1786, William Herschel was seated next to Mr Cavendish, who was reputed to be the most taciturn of men. Some time passed without his uttering a word, then he suddenly turned to his neighbour and said: 'I am told that you see the stars round, Dr Herschel'. 'Round as a button', was the reply. A long silence ensued till, towards the end of dinner, Cavendish again opened his lips to say in a doubtful voice: 'Round as a button?' 'Exactly, round as a button', repeated Herschel, and so the conversation ended.

From the diary of John Evelyn, 27 January 1658:

After six fits of a quartan ague with which it pleased God to visit him, died my deare son Richard, to our inexpressible griefe and affliction, 5 yeares and 3 days old onely, but at that tender age a prodigy for witt and understanding; for beauty of body a very angel; for endowment of mind of incredible and rare hopes. To give onely a little taste of some of them, and thereby glory to God, who out of the mouths of babes and infants does sometimes perfect his praises: at 2 yeares and halfe old he could perfectly reade any of the English, Latine, French, or Gothic letters, pronouncing the three first languages exactly. He had before the fifth yeare, or in that yeare, not onely skill to reade most written hands, but to decline all the nouns, conjugate the verbs regular, and most of the irregular; learn'd out Puerilis, got by heart almost the entire vocabularie of Latine and French primitives and words, could make congruous syntax, turne English into Latine, and vice versa, construe and prove what he read, and did the government and use of relatives, verbs, substantives, elipses, and many figures and tropes, and made a considerable progress in Comenius's *Janua*; began himselfe to write legibly, and had a strong passion for Greeke.

Regular Cracker readers will be aware how many items I owe to the serendipity of my friend John Yeoman. He died, alas, some months ago; here, recorded in his memory, is one of his favourite couplets. It comes from Scene ix of David and Bathsheba, *by George Peele; the speaker is Absalom:*

> His thunder is entangled in my hair,
> And with my beauty is his lightning quenched.

In 1606 the King of Denmark paid a state visit to the court of James I, where a masque was performed in his honour. Among those present was Sir John Harington, who described it afterwards:

One day a great feast was held, and after dinner the representation of Solomon his Temple and the coming of the Queen of Sheba was made, before their Majesties, by device of the Earl of Salisbury and others. – But alas! as all earthly thinges do fail to poor mortals in enjoyment, so did prove our presentment hereof. The Lady who did play the Queen's part did carry most precious gifts to both their Majesties; but forgetting the steppes arising to the canopy, overset her caskets into his Danish Majestie's lap, and fell at his feet, tho I rather think it was in his face. Much was the hurry and confusion; cloths and napkins were at hand to make all clean. His Majesty then got up and would dance with the Queen of Sheba; but he fell down and humbled himself before her, and was carried to an inner chamber and laid on a bed of state; which was not a little defiled with the presents of the Queen which had been bestowed on his garments; such as wine, cream, jelly, beverage, cakes, spices and other good matters. The entertainment and shew went forward and most of the presenters went backward, or fell down, wine did so occupy their upper chambers. Now did appear in rich dress Hope, Faith and Charity: Hope did assay to speak, but wine rendered her endeavours so feeble that she withdrew, and hoped the King would excuse her brevity. Faith was then all alone, for I am certain she was not joyned with good works; and left the Court in a staggering condition. Charity came to the King's feet, and seemed to cover the multitude of sins her sisters had committed: In some sorte she made obeysance and brought giftes, but said she would return home again, as there was no gift which Heaven had not already given his Majesty; she then returned to Hope and Faith, who were both sick and spewing in the lower hall.

Next came *Victory*, in bright armour, and presented a rich sword to the King, who did not accept it, but put it by with his hand; and, by a strange medley of versification, did endeavour to make suit to the King; but Victory did not tryumph for long, for, after much lamentable utterance, she was led away like a silly captive, and laid to sleep in the outer steps of the antechamber. Now did Peace make entry, and strive to get foremoste to the King; but I grieve to tell how great wrath she did discover unto those of her attendants, and, much contrary to her own semblance, most rudely made war with her olive branch, and laid on the pates of those who did oppose her coming. I have much marvelled at these strange pageantries, and they do bring to my remembrance what passed of this sort in our Queens days; of which I was sometime a humble presenter and assistant; but I neer did see such lack of good order, discretion, and sobriety, as I have now done . . .

It is no good going to bed early to save candles if the result be twins.

Chinese proverb

In his superb Parodies, *Dwight Macdonald tells of his doubts when he first came across – in* New Directions 14 *– the essay by Dr Rudolph Friedmann which follows: 'Was it a parody? Indeed, was there an actual Dr Friedmann? I have recently written to him and the answers are no and yes. (My letter explained that I wanted to use his piece in an anthology of parodies.)' He goes on to quote Dr Friedmann's reply: 'The article was written as a serious analytical–literary contribution . . . All my work is serious, although sometimes I use an aphoristic style to hammer home something that some writers take pages and pages to explain . . . You may certainly use the article.'*

Most of us, I suspect, are familiar with Struwwelpeter *in one way or another; many of us were brought up on it. And we have all recognized it as sick. But no one can ever have seen it as quite so sick as Dr Friedmann does, or have invested it with quite such a degree of sinister significance.*

STRUWWELPETER

Merry Stories and Funny Pictures

When the children have been good,
That is, be it understood,
Good at meal-times, good at play,
Good all night and good all day—
They shall have the pretty things
Merry Christmas always brings.

Naughty, romping girls and
    boys
Tear their clothes and make a
    noise,
Spoil their pinafores and frocks,
And deserve no Christmas-box.
Such as these shall never look
At this pretty Picture-book.

Shock-headed Peter

Just look at him! there he stands,
With his nasty hair and hands.
See! his nails are never cut;
They are grimed as black as soot;
And the sloven, I declare,
Never once has combed his hair;
Anything to me is sweeter
Than to see Shock-headed Peter.

AUTHOR'S NOTE: *Dr Heinrich Hoffman, the creator of Struwwelpeter (Shock-headed Peter or Slovenly Peter), was born on June 13, 1809 in Frankfurt-am-Main and studied medicine at Heidelberg, Halle and Paris; then became teacher of anatomy at the Senckenberg Foundation in Frankfurt. From 1851–89 he was house surgeon at the State Asylum, the building of which he first instituted. He died September 20, 1894 in Frankfurt. On the medical side he published* Observations and Experiences on Mental Disturbances in connection with Epilepsy *(1859). Dr Hoffman was best known for his illustrated children's books;* Struwwelpeter, *first published in 1845, went into many editions and was translated into almost all European languages. Similar books followed, like* King Nutcracker, In Heaven and on Earth, Bastian the Lazybones *(written under the pseudonym 'Polykarpus Gastfenger'); a satire called* Spar Salthole *(Badeort Salzloch, 1861), then a* Breviary of Marriage *(Leipzig, 1853);* Humoristic Studies *(1847) – in these studies there is included a comedy called* The Late-comers to the Moon *(Mondzügler). He also published in 1858* The Booklet of All Souls, *a humoristic cemetery anthology (Friedhofs-anthologie). But* Struwwelpeter *is the imago among his books.*

The title page of *Struwwelpeter* shows two Christmas angels dropping gifts from heaven to earth – for the little girl a doll and a cot, and, of course, the missing penis in the shape of an umbrella and a teapot; for the boy a smiling angel hopes he will come to some harm with a sword and a bayonet. In the lower center picture a child is eating and to the right there is a superb abstract study of a mother's back consisting of bonnet, pointed red shawl and crinoline, leading a child through a street of cobblestones and gothic spires. We turn over and encounter Struwwelpeter – Shock-headed Peter – and he really is a shock. He stands on a dais which has a design of open scissors let into its front. He contains in his own person all the elements running through the other characters in the book. He is a castrated child, grown fat as a result of glandular disturbance caused by the castration. His hair is a luminous halo of uncombed black and yellow out of which a frightened feminine face tries to gaze with schizoid severity and direction to compensate for the lost and holy genital eye which alone can see in the vagina of life and the coffin of death. There are stories that the penis still moves in the first few days sojourn in the cemetery and that bell-like drops of blood drip from the bud. The mop of hair also serves as a veil behind which the face may hide to avoid injury and the expression flies into some special introversion. To make up for the genital loss his outstretched hands possess five fingernails uncut and grown into five long sadistic claws sharp like erect tails. And yet the claws are no longer really cruel, there is only a façade of cruelty. The whole growing pyknic obesity of the figure gives the nails a self-crucifying and drooping look; just as the hair at its ends curls again inwards and downwards onto the breast of introversion. There are no life-lines or heart-lines in these outstretched hands, only stigmata forming little folds of death. The whole figure, dating from 1845, as one is moved by its mute message to unveil it, is a tragic commentary on the impending fate of the German nation.

Struwwelpeter himself is followed by a regression in time to the period of his phallic flowering as Cruel Frederick. The top illustration shows Frederick, with body erect, shouting. Shouting is a symbolical form of sexual aggression in which the voice is used as a substitute for the penis. In this picture the thin whiplash howl of the boy is directed against the nurse (the mother-imago in the form of the nurse) and has to do with the recognition that by giving birth to the son the mother has shown herself to be an animal. In this connection one is reminded of Christ's constant aggression against his own mother deriving from the fact that his unconscious did not believe her to be a virgin. Brandishing a chair over his head Frederick overturns a cage and kills the two birds which were in it; a small bird (the innocent tender white penis) and a large bird, its neck already heavily suffused with the sticky blood of masturbation. He tears the wings off flies (my genital hopes cannot soar; therefore yours shall not), kills the kitten with a brick and, in the farthest right-hand corner of the picture, as a frantic child far smaller than she, proceeds to whip his Mary (the mother of Christ). The son's hatred for the mother arises because she is a castrated being who has not got a penis to take off and give to him so that he may have a spare one handy after the father has done his work. (Cf. 'Woman, I know thee not,' with its frank expression of unconcern for the mother with whom the son has not had sexual intercourse and whose body He has thus not been able to explore to learn if it conceals a penis.) Frederick then proceeds to whip his dog Tray (amidst a wonderful setting of mountainous hills and gothic church spire) and ultimately is put to bed after the roused dog has bitten his leg.

There follows the story of Harriet and the matches; Harriet lights a match and her doll, which she has dropped, rushes out of the bottom corner of the illustration with flying petticoats. Harriet's apron-strings catch fire and the chorus of two crying cats, looking like two rats (the double penis she would not wait for, preferring the flame-like love which is as death to the young girl) send a stream of water to fertilize her two little scarlet shoes which is all that is left of her.

The Inky Boys (to begin with quite white) breathe out racial hatred for Black-a-moor symbolizing the exotic sinfulness of African and

Asiatic potency. But the punishing father and still living German super-ego, Agrippa, lived close by, 'so tall he almost touched the sky';

> 'He had a mighty inkstand, too,
> In which a great goose-feather grew.'

(Cf. The long thin, almost imperceptible, black hair growing out of the middle of the palm of the left hand of masturbators.)* Agrippa drops the three horrors into the inkstand so that they emerge blacker than Black-a-moor. The three are thrown back into the black well of the mother's womb to be reminded of their origin. 'Inter urinas et faeces nascimur.'

There follows a curious interlude, 'The Story of the Man that went out Shooting.' A man out hunting falls asleep in the warm smiling sun and has his gun stolen by the hare he is hunting. The man dreams and sees the hare pointing the gun at his anus. Through the magic of the drawing he seems to be facing both front and back simultaneously as he flees. And just as he reaches the safety of the mother through falling down a well, the hare fires and misses him. Struwwelpeter flirts with homosexuality but wakes up in time to save his virginity.

In 'The Story of Little Suck-a-Thumb' the analyst in Hoffman breaks through, with the fire of the first and last world, the veil of nineteenth-century repression. The first illustration is framed by the heads of two fathers; the motif of pointed beard and two eyes intertwined is repeated in the abstract pattern of a Cross inside a beard down both sides of the picture in which Conrad is being warned not to suck his thumb (not to masturbate) while his mother is out, as:

> 'The great tall tailor always comes
> To little boys who suck their thumbs;
> And ere they dream what he's about,
> He takes his great sharp scissors out,
> And cuts their thumbs clean off – and then,
> You know, they never grow again.'

The moment Mamma has turned her back Conrad's thumb is in his mouth (the child is sexually stimulated by the prohibition coming from the mother), and at the top of the second picture the frowning father surveys him from the wall. In rushes 'the great, long, red-legged scissor-man' and cuts off both thumbs with snip-snap slashes amidst a

---

* Footnote by Dwight MacDonald: When I reached this point on rereading this piece, certain doubts as to either Mr Friedmann's sanity or mine became inescapable. I began to wonder if the author means there *is* such a 'long, thin, almost imperceptible black hair' on masturbators' palms, or if he is referring to an erroneous folk belief. The style suggests the former and this suspicion swelled monstrously – one can imagine what Mr Friedmann would do with *that* image – as I read on and on . . . and on. We live in a very strange intellectual world these days. And why the *left* hand? No, my dear Friedmann, please don't explain.

pool of blood. And in the final illustration the father beams down with deep ripe pleasure at castrated Conrad. This story, in its illumination of the nuances of life, is as great a contribution to world literature as is Goethe's *Faust*. To Schiller's maxim that 'Hunger and Love make the world go round,' can be added 'and Castration stops it'.

The first illustration of 'The Story of Augustus who would not have any Soup' shows a boy in whom the pyknic disposition is only sustained by food; in the four subsequent illustrations (even including the end which is schizoid through and through in its heartless realistic irony) the innate dynamism towards nothingness of Northern schizoid tendencies is revealed in all its melting pathos. This schizophrenia contains a very real dynamism both of body and mind; in contrast to the degenerate European schizophrenia of today with its well-developed rigidity of movement and thought with consequent tomb-like facial expression which has become a substitute for the grandeur of the schizoid imago. However, 'The Story of Augustus' is essentially the story of the boy who is so sickened by his own masturbatory excretions that he cannot bear the sight of soup. Through excessive masturbation he becomes thinner and thinner until – on the fifth day – he dies. The final illustration shows a tureen marked 'soup' lying against a Cross. The correctness of Hoffman's viewpoint is borne out by the fact that analysis is more and more returning to the folk-viewpoint that excessive masturbation leads to early death. This is especially the case among biologically degenerate men whose bony tissue is gradually wasted away.

The masturbatory theme is continued with 'The Story of Fidgety Philip', who rocks himself to and fro until he topples over onto the floor and pulls the tablecloth and the contents of the table down upon himself so that he is covered in white sauce! In the final illustration a pendant bird hangs prophetically amongst knives and a broken bottle.

'The Story of Johnny Head-In-Air' shows Johnny so busy masturbating that he becomes blind, cannot see where he is going, collides with an aggressive dog (the father), and falls over the river embankment which is lighted by a curious lamppost. In the next illustration the boy lies face downward, half drowned, in the water and only the base of the lamppost is visible, the top being snapped off by the angle of the drawing. He is then hooked out by two strong men.

The final 'Story of Flying Robert' ends this essentially tragic book. Robert leaves his home, in spite of all commands to stay indoors on windy days, opens his red umbrella and is at once borne away on the wind into the Unknown. It consists of three pictures ('3' – the number which is lucky because it contains in its ancient Hebrew hieroglyphic form the shape of the penis). Robert has masturbated so copiously and become so light that as soon as he raises his umbrella he is swept off the face of the earth. He lacks all ballast because his parents have cut off his genitals and made giblet soup of them. The death of the child is the birth of the parents. Although flying free, Robert was sucked along the avenue leading up to the opening of death and his dead head banged against the sky. 'Is it very hot and afterwards very lonely.' His head is presented to death and the ashes of the past are thrown over him to acclimatize the ashes of the future. As Robert is borne aloft on the phantasy wings of his last erection there is no more movement on earth, only a packed swaying in a drawn circle.

Struwwelpeter recognizes and gives expression to the sexuality and criminality of the child; in the case of the little girl, the wish to set fire to her genitals; in the case of the boy, masturbation inspired by cruelty to animals and to the mother together with the self-realization that castration is the only cure for him. In consequence the nineteenth-century child was healthily repressed. Woe betide those who weaken the super-ego amongst primitives (and the child is a degenerate primitive). Only after castration does the son feel ready to receive the father's blessing. Arising out of the tendency to substitute analysis for repression in our dealings with the intellectually unripe, the tremendous growth of contemporary aggression is best exemplified by reference to a phrase from the court of linguistics; in a former age to 'do' someone meant to cheat them financially; now it means to injure their genital organs with a razor.

The best in *Struwwelpeter* represents the psychology of distance made into human art through a nearness to the natural. And it is essentially modern in its outlook because it reveals the child's need for sexual expression; indeed the child who does not experience sexuality now may find that it will lose its virginity to the atom bomb and not to man. Struwwelpeter is like a boil, or a nipple bursting with milk; he represents the expression of a repression and his swollen larger-than-life appearance is a symbolic representation of the painful, blocked orgasm and the phantasy of pregnancy in childhood.

The book is closed and the cover faces us. The schizoid talons and the shadows of the feet overcome the pyknic obesity of the figure, and the eyes searching the woman-reader separate the animal in her from the imago. But Struwwelpeter is not concerned with life; the finding of the warm instinctive animal side of the woman does not heal him or stimulate him creatively; on the contrary he whips and destroys her. Whereas originally, at least, his aggression sprang from interest in life, today Struwwelpeter cannot visualize life and has no interest in it; he is a shot and reeling monument to the whiteness of the way where good and bad youth treads carefully to death.

Acknowledgements: The author and publishers are grateful to the following for permission to quote extracts.

David Higham Associates Ltd for 'Do not go gentle into that good night' by Dylan Thomas; Ian Allan Ltd for *Nineteenth Century Railway Carriages* by Hamilton Ellis (London 1949); Chatto & Windus and Oxford University Press for *Wilfred Owen* by Jon Stallworthy (1974); Collins Publishers for *Companion Guide to Devon and Cornwall* by Sir Darrell Bates; Curtis Brown Group Ltd on behalf of the Estate of W. H. Auden and Louis MacNeice for *Letters From Iceland*, Faber 1937; *Connoisseur* magazine for 'William Beckford's Library' by Anthony Hobson, April 1976; James Lees-Milne for *Beckford at Fonthill*; Faber & Faber for 'And love hung still' from *Trilogy for X* by Louis MacNeice; Nerissa Martin for letter by Nevill Coghill to Stewart Perowne (1970); Professor Quentin Bell for extract from *The Diary of Virginia Woolf*, September 1916; Curtis Brown (N.Y.) Ltd for 'All the Days of Christmas' by Phyllis McGinley, © 1958 by the Hearst Corporation; Elaine Greene Ltd for 'Twelfth Night; or, What Will You Have?' by Michael Frayn; A. D. Peters & Co. Ltd for *Labels* by Evelyn Waugh; William Heinemann for *Jerusalem* by Colin Thubron; Duckworth and Viking (U.S.) for *Collected Dorothy Parker*; Longman Group U.K. Ltd for *Clio, A Muse* by G. M. Trevelyan; Grafton for *Waterhouse at Large* by Keith Waterhouse; Faber & Faber for *Collected Poems* by W. H. Auden; The Estate of Hilaire Belloc for 'Song in the Old Manner'; Faber & Faber for *The Violent Effigy: A Study of Dickens* by John Carey; Collins Publishers for *The Peregrine* by J. A. Baker; John Murray for *On the Edge of Paradise* by David Newsome; Roy Dean for 'Word Row'; David Higham Associates Ltd for *Biography of Alexander Pope* by Edith Sitwell; The Literary Estate of the late Sir Charles Johnston for *The Hatchery*; John Murray for *The Lyttelton/Hart Davis Letters*; Auberon Waugh for extracts from letters by Evelyn Waugh; Maurice Baring for *Dead Letters* and *A Number of People*; The Literary Estate of Victoria Sackville-West for 'Sometimes, when night has thickened in the woods'; A. P. Watt Ltd on behalf of the Executors of the Estate of C. L. Dodgson for 'Wasp in the Wig' (unpublished) extract from *Through the Looking Glass*; Francis Day & Hunter for lyrics to ''Arold And Others' by Marriott Edgar; Constable Publishers for *Medieval Latin Lyrics* by Helen Waddell; Oxford University Press for *Oxford Guide to Oxford* by Peter Heyworth (1981); A. P. Watt Ltd on behalf of the Executors of the Estate of Robert Graves for 'With the Gift of Rings'; Curtis Brown Ltd for *Painting As A Pastime* by Winston

Churchill; Faber & Faber for 'The Horses' from *The Collected Poems of Edwin Muir*; William Heinemann Ltd for 'The Jewel in the Crown' from *The Raj Quartet* by Paul Scott; Oxford University Press for *The Notebooks of Geoffrey Madan*, edited by John Sparrow and J. A. Gere (1981).

Index

Authors of substantive items are listed in CAPITALS